Easy Timeless Quilts

LEISURE ARTS, INC. • Maumelle, Arkansas

EDITORIAL STAFF
Senior Product Director: Pam Stebbins
Creative Art Director: Katherine Laughlin
Publications Director: Leah Lampirez
Technical Editor: Lisa Lancaster
Editorial Writer: Susan Frantz Wiles
Art Category Manager: Lora Puls
Graphic Artist: Cailen Cochran
Prepress Technician: Stephanie Johnson
Contributing Photography Stylist: Sondra Daniels
Contributing Photographer: Ken West

BUSINESS STAFF
President and Chief Executive Officer: Fred F. Pruss
Senior Vice President of Operations: Jim Dittrich
Vice President of Retail Sales: Martha Adams
Chief Financial Officer: Tiffany P. Childers
Controller: Teresa Eby
Information Technology Director: Brian Roden
Director of E-Commerce: Mark Hawkins
Manager of E-Commerce: Robert Young

Copyright © 2015 by Leisure Arts, Inc., 104 Champs Blvd., STE 100, Maumelle, AR 72113-6738, www.leisurearts.com. All rights reserved. This publication is protected under federal copyright laws. Reproduction or distribution of this publication or any other Leisure Arts publication, including publications which are out of print, is prohibited unless specifically authorized. This includes, but is not limited to, any form of reproduction or distribution on or through the Internet, including posting, scanning, or e-mail transmission. We have made every effort to ensure that these instructions are accurate and complete. We cannot, however, be responsible for human error, typographical mistakes, or variations in individual work.

ISBN-13/EAN: 978-1-4647-4330-6

UPC: 0-28906-06653-1

Made in U.S.A.

introduction

With their charming fabrics and patterns that stir memories, quilts offer a timeless way to add warmth to today's home. This book presents a special collection of seven classic quilts that are easy to make using modern techniques such as rotary cutting and strip piecing.

Even if you are a beginner, the clear instructions and assembly diagrams will help you finish each quilt with ease! Discover all the fun and satisfaction of creating heirloom quilts for yourself and your loved ones. They'll never go out of style, and they'll enrich your home today, tomorrow, and for many years to come.

table of contents

plaid quilt

This super-easy quilt features simple four-patch blocks and plain setting squares, all tied with embroidery floss for a quick finish. The cozy look of plaids and stripes will make this blanket a family favorite. It's a great pattern for when you're needing a gift in a hurry.

FINISHED BLOCK SIZE: 16 1/2" x 16 1/2" (42 cm x 42 cm)
FINISHED QUILT SIZE: 83 1/2" x 100" (212 cm x 254 cm)

YARDAGE REQUIREMENTS

Yardage is based on 43"/44" (109 cm/112 cm) wide fabric with a usable width of 40" (102 cm).

4 5/8 yds (4.2 m) **total** of assorted dark plaids (our quilt uses 11 different dark plaids)

4 3/8 yds (4 m) **total** of assorted light plaids and stripes (our quilt uses 9 different light plaids and stripes)

7 5/8 yds (7 m) of fabric for backing

1 yd (91 cm) of fabric for binding

91 1/2" x 108" (232 cm x 274 cm) piece of batting

You will also need:
Black embroidery floss

20 black 1" (25 mm) buttons

CUTTING THE PIECES

Follow ***Rotary Cutting****, page 40, to cut fabric. Cut all strips across the selvage-to-selvage width of the fabric. All measurements include 1/4" seam allowances.*

from assorted dark plaids:

- Cut 46 **strips** 3 1/4"w.

from assorted light plaids and stripes:

- Cut 135 **squares** 6" x 6".

— using plaids and stripes —

Mixing lots of stripes and plaids in a single project is not as difficult as you might think when you keep the following guidelines in mind:

Think about plaids and stripes as you would any other fabric.

- Do your plaids and stripes fall into pleasing color families?
- Do you have a variety of scales in your fabrics? Are some plaids large-scale and some smaller scale? Is the same true for your striped fabrics?
- Will some of your fabrics "act like" background fabrics, while others may be bolder "feature fabrics?"

Cutting plaids and stripes doesn't have to be an ordeal either.

- If your plaids and stripes are woven, take care to align your cuts carefully with the grain of the fabric.
- If your fabrics are printed, consider aligning your cuts with the "visual grainline" — the straight lines of the design — even if the design doesn't match the true fabric grain.
- Or, you may ignore the "visual grainline" of printed fabrics altogether. Many of today's scrappy projects get their old-fashioned charm from plaids and stripes with designs that "veer off" the edges of the cut pieces.

Sterling & Noble
CLOCK COMPANY
QUARTZ
THE DANCE

ASSEMBLING THE QUILT TOP

*Follow **Machine Piecing**, page 40, and **Pressing**, page 41. To achieve the scrappy look of our quilt, assemble strips, squares, and units in random fabric combinations. Use a 1/4" seam allowance.*

1. Assemble **strips** as shown to make **Strip Set A**. Make 23 Strip Set A's. Cut across Strip Set A's at 3 1/4" intervals to make **Unit 1**. Make 270 Unit 1's.

Strip Set A (make 23)

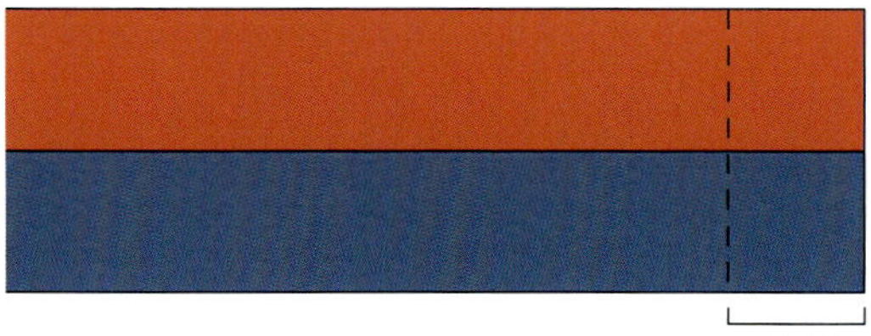

Unit 1 (make 270)

2. Assemble 2 **Unit 1's** as shown to make **Unit 2**. Make 135 Unit 2's.

Unit 2 (make 135)

3. Assemble 2 **squares** and 1 **Unit 2** as shown to make **Unit 3**. Make 45 Unit 3's. Assemble 2 **Unit 2's** and 1 **square** as shown to make **Unit 4**. Make 45 Unit 4's.

Unit 3 (make 45)

Unit 4 (make 45)

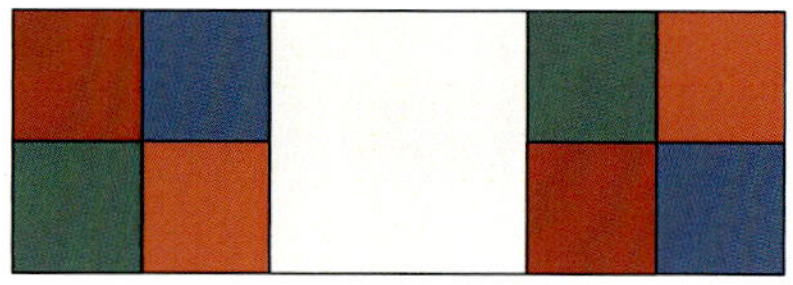

4. Assemble 2 **Unit 3's** and 1 **Unit 4** as shown to make **Block A**. Make 15 Block A's. Assemble 2 **Unit 4's** and 1 **Unit 3** as shown to make **Block B**. Make 15 Block B's.

Block A (make 15)

Block B (make 15)

5. Referring to Assembly Diagram and alternating **Blocks**, sew Blocks together into rows. Rotating rows as necessary, sew rows together to complete **Quilt Top**.

COMPLETING THE QUILT

1. Follow Tying A Quilt, page 44, to layer and tie quilt. Tie quilt at outside corners of Unit 2's. Before trimming floss ends, refer to Assembly Diagram to attach buttons to corners of Blocks.
2. Cut a 33" square of binding fabric. Follow Making Continuous Bias Strip Binding, page 46, to make $2^1/_2$"w bias binding.
3. Follow Attaching Binding with Overlapped Corners, page 48, to attach binding to quilt.

Assembly Diagram

double nine-patch quilt

The blocks of the Double Nine-Patch are amazingly simple to piece, yet the pattern they create when set "on point" with plain setting squares seems complex. Because there are setting triangles on the ends of each row and on the four corners, this is an excellent first quilt for learning how to cut and sew triangles. The border has mitered corners, a basic technique that creates a professional-looking finish.

FINISHED BLOCK SIZE: 11¹/₄" x 11¹/₄" (29 cm x 29 cm)
FINISHED QUILT SIZE: 75³/₄" x 75³/₄" (192 cm x 192 cm)

Our instructions eliminate bias edges and substitute a small red print for the checked fabric. The maker of our antique quilt dealt with many bias edges in order to match the direction of the checks in her quilt top.

YARDAGE REQUIREMENTS

Yardage is based on 43"/44" (109 cm/112 cm) wide fabric with a usable width of 40" (102 cm).

5 yds (4.6 m)
of red print fabric

3³/₈ yds (3.1 m)
of navy print fabric

7 yds (6.4 m)
of fabric for backing

1 yd (91 cm)
of fabric for binding

84" x 84"
(213 cm x 213 cm)
piece of batting

CUTTING THE PIECES

*Follow **Rotary Cutting**, page 40, to cut fabric. Cut all strips across the selvage-to-selvage width of the fabric unless otherwise indicated. All measurements include ¹/₄" seam allowances.*

from red print:

- Cut 16 **strips** 1³/₄" wide.
- Cut 8 strips 4¹/₄"w. From these strips, cut 64 **squares** 4¹/₄" x 4¹/₄".
- Cut 4 *lengthwise* **outer borders** 3¹/₂" x 80".
- From remaining fabric:
  - Cut 9 **setting squares** 11³/₄" x 11³/₄".
  - Cut 2 squares 8⁷/₈" x 8⁷/₈". Cut squares once diagonally to make 4 **corner setting triangles**.
  - Cut 3 squares 17¹/₄" x 17¹/₄". Cut each square twice diagonally to make 12 **side setting triangles**.

from navy print:

- Cut 20 **strips** 1³/₄" wide.
- Cut 4 *lengthwise* **inner borders** 3" x 80".

ASSEMBLING THE QUILT TOP

*Follow **Machine Piecing**, page 40, and **Pressing**, page 41. Use a $^{1}/_{4}$" seam allowance.*

1. Sew 2 navy **strips** and 1 red **strip** together to make **Strip Set A**. Make 8 Strip Set A's. Cut across Strip Set A's at $1^{3}/_{4}$" intervals to make 160 **Unit 1's**.

Strip Set A
(make 8)

Unit 1
(make 160)

2. Sew 2 red **strips** and 1 navy **strip** together to make **Strip Set B**. Make 4 **Strip** Set B's. Cut across Strip Set B's at $1^{3}/_{4}$" intervals to make 80 **Unit 2's**.

Strip Set B
(make 4)

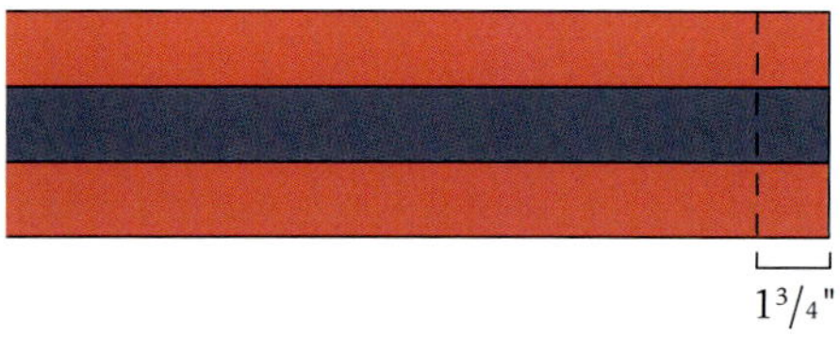

Unit 2
(make 80)

3. Sew 2 **Unit 1's** and 1 **Unit 2** together to make **Unit 3**. Make 80 Unit 3's.

Unit 3 (make 80)

4. Sew 2 **Unit 3's** and 1 **square** together to make **Unit 4**. Make 32 Unit 4's.

Unit 4 (make 32)

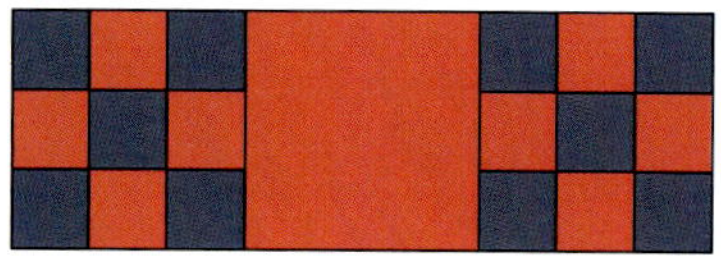

5. Sew 2 **squares** and 1 **Unit 3** together to make **Unit 5**. Make 16 Unit 5's.

Unit 5 (make 16)

6. Sew 2 **Unit 4's** and 1 **Unit 5** together to make Block. Make 16 Blocks.

Block (make 16)

7. Referring to Assembly Diagram, page 12, sew **corner setting triangles**, **side setting triangles**, **Blocks**, and **setting squares** together into diagonal rows. Sew rows together to make center section of quilt top.

8. Sew 1 **inner border** and 1 **outer border** together to make Border Unit. Make 4 Border Units.

Border Units (make 4)

9. Referring to Quilt Top Diagram, page 13, follow Adding Mitered Borders, page 42, to sew **Border Units** to center section to complete **Quilt Top**.

COMPLETING THE QUILT

1. Follow Quilting, page 42, to mark, layer, and quilt. Our quilt is hand quilted.
2. Cut a 30" square of binding fabric. Follow Making Continuous Bias Strip Binding, page 46, to make $2^1/_2$"w bias binding.
3. Follow Attaching Binding With Mitered Corners, page 46, to attach binding to quilt.

Assembly Diagram

Quilt Top Diagram

triple irish chain quilt

One of the oldest block patterns, the Irish Chain design was developed from a simple shape—the square. This Triple Irish Chain quilt is pieced in strong solid colors that are reminiscent of the designs traditionally made by the Amish craftswomen of Ohio. The geometric form and bold colors are as well-suited to the modern home as they were to households of the past.

FINISHED BLOCK SIZE: $10\frac{1}{2}$" x $10\frac{1}{2}$" (27 cm x 27 cm)
FINISHED QUILT SIZE: $89\frac{1}{4}$" x $99\frac{3}{4}$" (227 cm x 253 cm)

YARDAGE REQUIREMENTS

Yardage is based on 43"/44" (109 cm/112 cm) wide fabric.

$5\frac{1}{8}$ yds (4.7 m)
of navy solid fabric

$3\frac{5}{8}$ yds (3.3 m)
of purple solid fabric

$2\frac{3}{8}$ yds (2.2 m)
of red solid fabric

$2\frac{1}{8}$ yds (1.9 m)
of teal solid fabric

$8\frac{1}{8}$ yds (7.4 m)
of fabric for backing

$1\frac{1}{8}$ yds (1 m)
of fabric for binding

$97\frac{1}{4}$" x $107\frac{3}{4}$" (247 cm x 274 cm)
piece of batting

CUTTING THE PIECES

*Follow **Rotary Cutting**, page 40, to cut fabric. Cut all strips across the selvage-to-selvage width of the fabric unless otherwise indicated. All measurements include $^{1}/_{4}$" seam allowances.*

from navy solid fabric:

- Cut 3 strips 8"w. From these strips, cut 15 **squares** 8" x 8".
- Cut 18 **strips** 2"w.
- Cut 4 **strips** 5"w.
- Cut 2 *lengthwise* **top/bottom outer borders** 9" x $92^{3}/_{4}$".
- Cut 2 *lengthwise* **side outer borders** 9" x $86^{1}/_{4}$".

from purple solid fabric:

- Cut 20 **strips** 2"w.
- Cut 2 *lengthwise* **side middle borders** 2" x $83^{1}/_{4}$".
- Cut 2 *lengthwise* **top/bottom middle borders** 2" x $75^{3}/_{4}$".
- Cut 2 *lengthwise* **side inner borders** 2" x $67^{1}/_{2}$".
- Cut 2 *lengthwise* **top/bottom inner borders** 2" x 60".

from red solid fabric:

- Cut 38 **strips** 2"w.

from teal solid fabric:

- Cut 34 **strips** 2"w.

ASSEMBLING THE QUILT TOP

*Follow **Machine Piecing**, page 40, and **Pressing**, page 41. Use a $^{1}/_{4}$" seam allowance.*

1. Assemble 2"w **strips** to make **Strip Set A**. Make 2 Strip Set A's. Cut across Strip Set A's at 2" intervals to make 30 **Unit 1's**.
2. Assemble 2"w **strips** to make **Strip Set B**. Make 2 Strip Set B's. Cut across Strip Set B's at 2" intervals to make 30 **Unit 2's**.
3. Assemble 2"w **strips** to make **Strip Set C**. Make 2 Strip Set C's. Cut across Strip Set C's at 2" intervals to make 30 **Unit 3's**.
4. Assemble 2"w **strips** to make **Strip Set D**. Cut across Strip Set D at 2" intervals to make 15 **Unit 4's**.

Strip Set A (make 2) **Unit 1** (make 30)

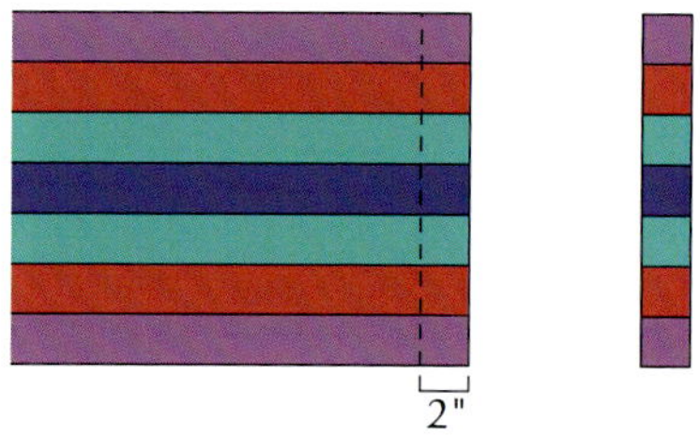

Strip Set B (make 2) **Unit 2** (make 30)

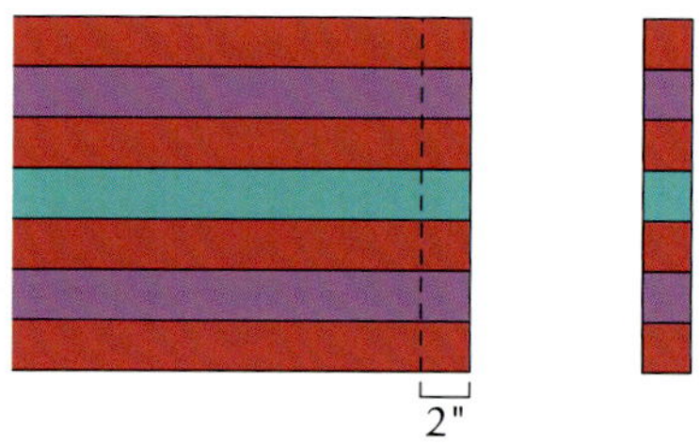

Strip Set C (make 2) **Unit 3** (make 30)

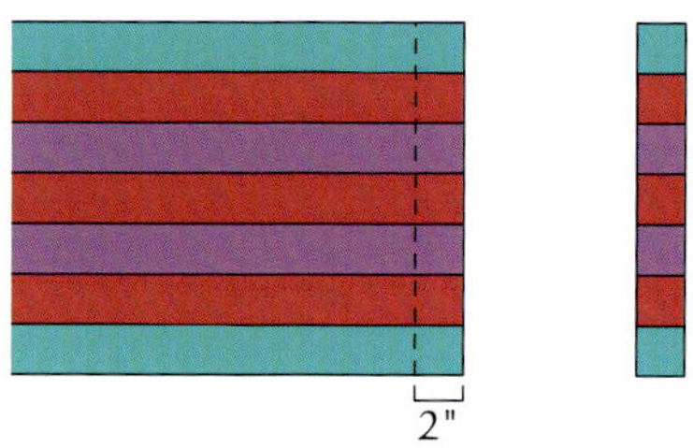

Strip Set D **Unit 4** (make 15)

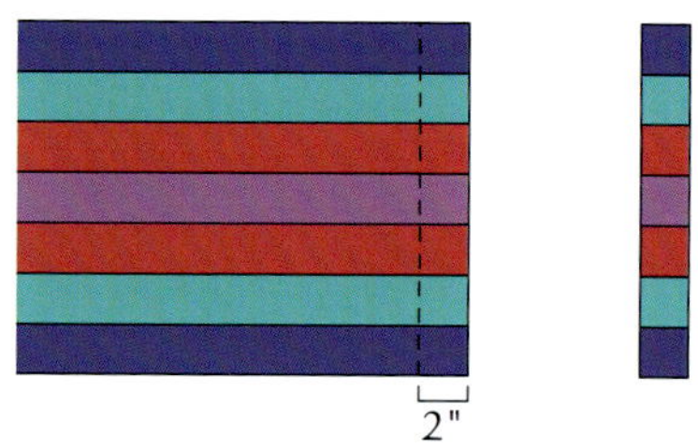

5. Assemble 2"w **strips** and 5"w **strip** to make Strip Set E. Make 2 Strip Set E's. Cut across **Strip Set E's** at 2" intervals to make 30 Unit 5's.
6. Assemble 2"w **strips** and 5"w **strip** to make Strip Set F. Make 2 Strip Set F's. Cut across **Strip Set F's** at 2" intervals to make 30 Unit 6's.
7. Assemble 2"w **strips** to make Strip Set G. Make 7 Strip Set G's. Cut across **Strip Set G's** at 2" intervals to make 126 Border Units.
8. Assemble 2 **Unit 1's**, 2 **Unit 2's**, 2 **Unit 3's**, and 1 **Unit 4** to make Block A. Make 15 Block A's.
9. Assemble 2 **Unit 5's**, 1 **square**, and 2 **Unit 6's** to make Block B. Make 15 Block B's.
10. Assemble 3 **Block A's** and 2 **Block B's** to make Row A. Make 3 Row A's.
11. Assemble 3 **Block B's** and 2 **Block A's** to make Row B. Make 3 Row B's.
12. Referring to Quilt Top Diagram, page 19, assemble **Rows** to make center section of quilt top.

Strip Set E (make 2)

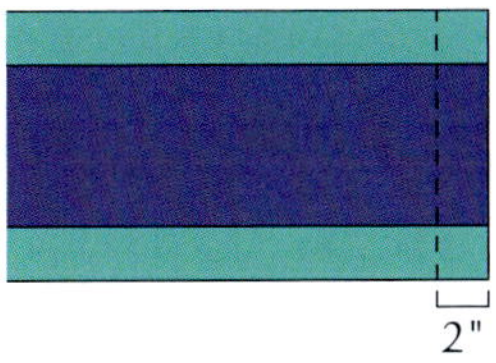

Unit 5 (make 30)

Strip Set F (make 2)

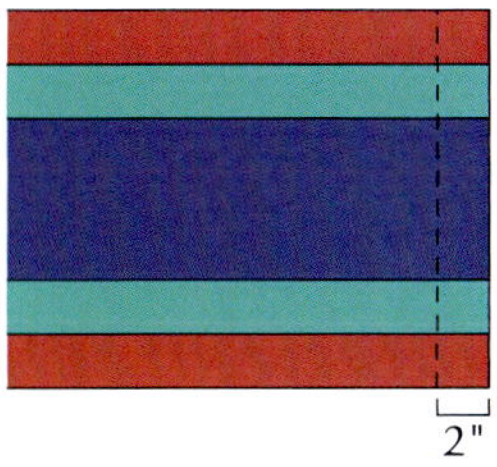

Unit 6 (make 30)

Strip Set G (make 7)

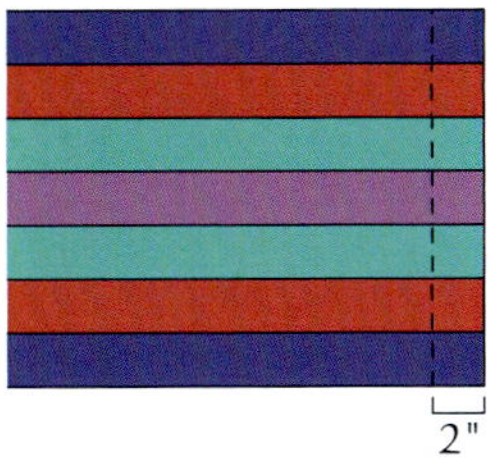

Border Unit (make 126)

Block A (make 15)

Block B (make 15)

Row A (make 3)

Row B (make 3)

13. Refer to Adding Squared Borders, page 41, to attach **side**, then **top** and **bottom inner borders** to center section of quilt top.
14. Use a seam ripper to take apart 12 **Border Units** to make 24 Partial Units as shown.
15. To make each Top/Bottom Seminole Patchwork Border, assemble 26 **Border Units**, then add 6 **Partial Units** to right end.
16. To make each Side Seminole Patchwork Border, assemble 31 **Border Units**, then add 6 **Partial Units** to right end.
17. Referring to Fig. 2, align 1/4" ruler marking (shown in pink) with outermost seam intersections and trim excess fabric from each long edge of each border to complete **Seminole Patchwork Borders**.
18. Easing borders to fit, sew **Seminole Patchwork Borders** to top, bottom, then sides of center section of quilt top, beginning and ending seams exactly 1/4" from each corner of quilt top and backstitching at beginning and end of stitching.
19. Fold 1 corner of quilt top diagonally with right sides together, matching outer edges of borders as shown in Fig. 3. Beginning at point where previous seams ended, stitch to outer corner. Repeat with remaining corners.
20. Follow Adding Squared Borders to attach **side**, then **top** and **bottom middle borders**. Attach **side**, then **top** and **bottom outer border** to complete **Quilt Top**.

Partial Units (make 24)

Top/Bottom Seminole Patchwork Border (make 2)

Side Seminole Patchwork Border (make 2)

Fig. 2

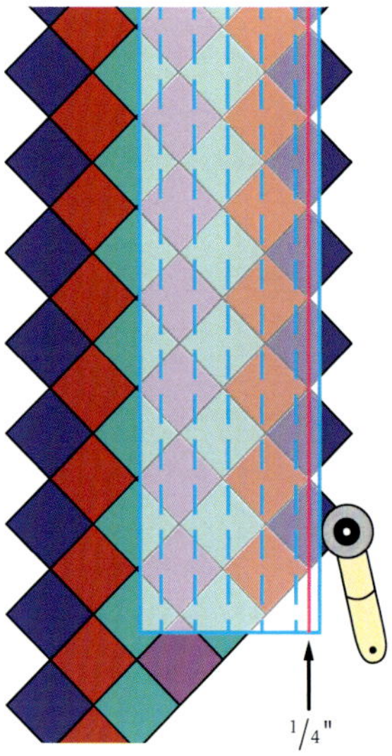

Fig. 3

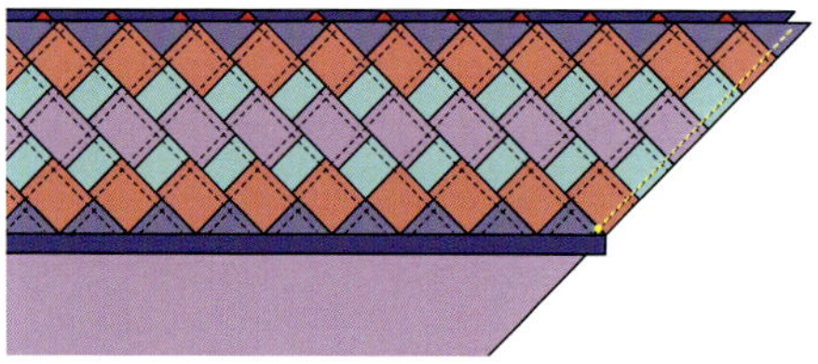

COMPLETING THE QUILT

1. Follow Quilting, page 42, to mark, layer, and quilt. Our quilt is hand quilted using classic cable, flower, and feather designs. The Block A's and the patchwork border are outline quilted along each seam. There are diagonal lines quilted around the flower in each Block B. The inner border is quilted with a cable design. The outer border has diagonal lines quilted around each feather design.
2. Cut a 34" square of binding fabric. Follow Binding, page 46, to bind quilt using $2^1/_2$"w bias binding with mitered corners.

Quilt Top Diagram

broken dishes quilt

The simplest of blocks can become the prettiest of quilts. This traditional beauty was made with small-scale prints from the late 1800s. To make a similar quilt for your modern home, choose reproduction fabrics. The red-white-and-blue color scheme will never go out of fashion, but the old-fashioned method of using templates to piece a quilt will probably remain a thing of the past. That's because today's quilters enjoy the greater ease and speed of using a rotary cutter and ruler to cut accurate triangles.

FINISHED BLOCK SIZE: 6½" x 6½" (17 cm x 17 cm)
FINISHED QUILT SIZE: 71½" x 84½" (182 cm x 215 cm)

YARDAGE REQUIREMENTS

Yardage is based on 43"/44" (109 cm/112 cm) wide fabric.

2½ yds (2.3 m)
of dark red print fabric

4 yds (3.7 m) total
of assorted dark print fabric scraps

4 yds (3.7 m) total
of assorted light print fabric scrap

5¼ yds (4.8 m)
of fabric for backing

1 yd (91 cm)
of fabric for binding

79½" x 92½" (202 cm x 235 cm)
piece of batting

You will also need:
Easy Angle™ Rotary Cutting Ruler
(made by EZ Quilting®)

CUTTING THE BORDERS

*Follow **Rotary Cutting**, page 40, to cut fabric. Cut all strips across the selvage-to-selvage width of the fabric unless otherwise indicated. All measurements include $^1/_4$" seam allowances.*

from dark red print:

- Cut 2 *lengthwise* **top/bottom borders** $3^1/_4$" x $69^1/_2$".
- Cut 2 *lengthwise* **side borders** $3^1/_4$" x 88".

Fig. 1

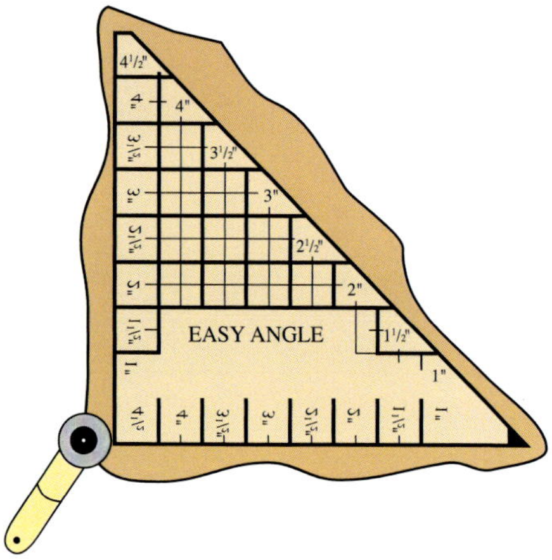

Fig. 2

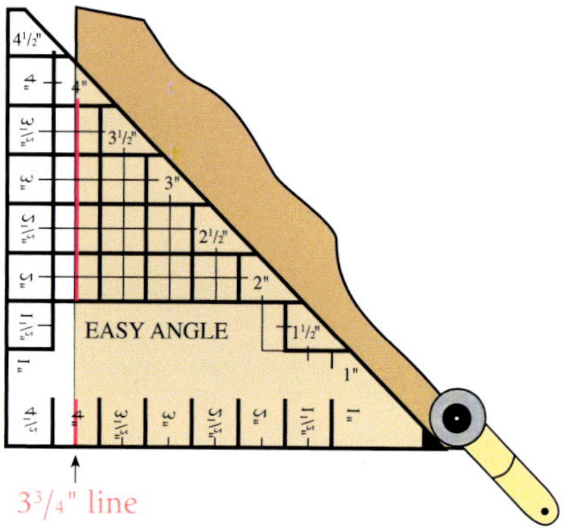

CUTTING THE TRIANGLES

1. To cut triangles, refer to Fig. 1 to line up left edge of Easy Angle ruler with straight grain of 1 fabric scrap. Cut along bottom and left edges of ruler.
2. Referring to Fig. 2, line up bottom edge of ruler with bottom cut edge of fabric; slide ruler to left until $3^3/_4$" line (shown in pink) is aligned with left cut edge of fabric. Cut along angled edge of ruler to complete **triangle**.
3. Repeat Steps 1 and 2 with remaining scraps to cut a total of 480 dark triangles and 480 light triangles.

Dark Triangle (cut 480)

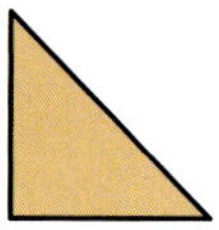

Light Triangle (cut 480)

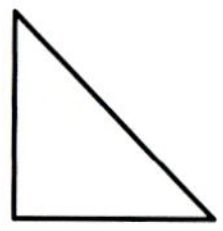

Triangle-Square (make 480)

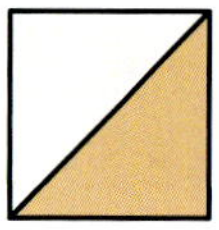

Block (make 120)

Row (make 12)

ASSEMBLING THE QUILT TOP

*Follow **Machine Piecing**, page 40, and **Pressing**, page 41. Use a $^1/_4$" seam allowance.*

1. Sew 1 **dark** and 1 **light triangle** together to make Triangle-Square. Make 480 triangle-squares.
2. Sew 4 **triangle-squares** together to make Block. Make 120 Blocks.

3. Sew 10 **Blocks** together to make Row. Make 12 Rows.
4. Referring to Quilt Top Diagram, sew **Rows** together to make center section of quilt top.
5. Follow Adding Squared Borders, page 41, to sew **top**, **bottom**, then **side borders** to center section to complete **Quilt Top.**

COMPLETING THE QUILT

1. Follow Quilting, page 42, to mark, layer, and quilt. Our quilt is hand quilted in diagonal lines.
2. Cut a 31" square of binding fabric. Follow Binding, page 46, to bind quilt using $2^1/_2$"w bias binding with overlapped corners.

Quilt Top Diagram

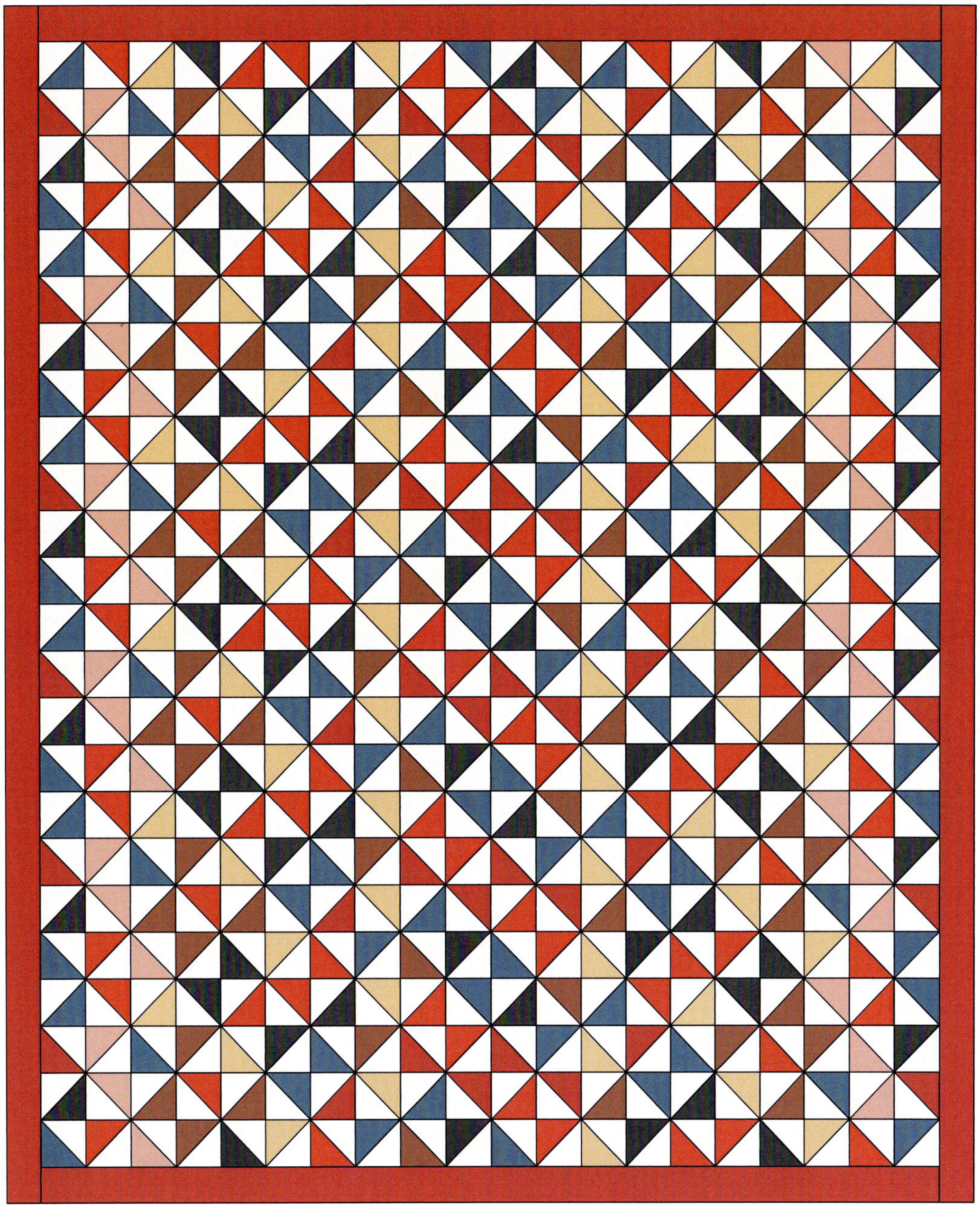

wild goose chase quilt

Wild Goose Chase is an easy-to-sew pattern that creates a dramatic quilt. When you use our fast and accurate method for creating the Flying Geese Units, you can create a vintage-style quilt that not only fits your home, but also your busy lifestyle.

FINISHED BLOCK SIZE: 12" x 12" (30 cm x 30 cm)
FINISHED QUILT SIZE: 78⅝" x 88⅝" (200 cm x 225 cm)

YARDAGE REQUIREMENTS

Yardage is based on 43"/44" (109 cm/112 cm) wide fabric.

5 yds (4.6 m) of brown print fabric for setting squares and triangles and outer borders

2 yds (1.8 m) total of assorted brown print fabrics for Flying Geese

2½ yds (2.3 m) total of assorted off-white print fabrics for Flying Geese

⅜ yd (34 cm) of pink print fabric for sashing squares and triangles

2½ yds (2.3 m) of off-white print fabric for unpieced inner borders [or ⅝ yd (57 cm) if piecing borders]

7¼ yds (6.6 m) of fabric for backing

1 yd (91 cm) of brown stripe fabric for binding

87" x 97" (221 cm x 246 cm) piece of batting

CUTTING THE PIECES

*Follow **Rotary Cutting**, page 40, to cut fabric. Cut all strips across the selvage-to-selvage width of the fabric. All measurements include 1/4" seam allowances.*

from brown print fabric:

- Cut 2 strips 18 1/4"w. From these strips, cut 4 squares 18 1/4" x 18 1/4". Cut each square twice diagonally to make 16 **side setting triangles** (you will use 13 and have 3 left over).
- Cut 2 *lengthwise* **side outer borders** 3" x 92".
- Cut 2 *lengthwise* **top/bottom outer borders** 3" x 77".
- From remaining fabric, cut *crosswise* strips 12 1/2"w. From these strips, cut 21 **setting squares** 12 1/2" x 12 1/2".
- Cut 1 square 9 3/8" x 9 3/8". Cut square once diagonally to make 2 **corner setting triangles**.

from assorted brown print fabrics:

- Cut 672 **rectangles** 1 1/2" x 2 1/2".

from assorted off-white print fabrics:

- Cut 1344 **squares** 1 1/2" x 1 1/2".

from pink print fabric:

- Cut 2 strips 2 1/2"w. From these strips, cut 21 **sashing squares** 2 1/2" x 2 1/2".
- Cut 1 strip 4 1/8"w. From this strip, cut 4 squares 4 1/8" x 4 1/8". Cut each square twice diagonally to make 16 **side sashing triangles** (you will use 13 and have 3 left over).
- Cut 1 square 2 3/8" x 2 3/8". Cut square once diagonally to make 2 **corner sashing triangles**.

from off-white print fabric for inner borders:

(2 1/2 yds)

- Cut 2 *lengthwise* **top/bottom inner borders** 2" x 74".
- Cut 2 *lengthwise* **side inner borders** 2" x 87".

OR

(5/8 yd)

- Cut 9 strips 2"w. Piece and trim strips to make 2 **top/bottom inner borders** 2" x 74" and 2 **side inner borders** 2" x 87".

ASSEMBLING THE QUILT TOP

*Follow **Machine Piecing**, page 40, and **Pressing**, page 41. Use a 1/4" seam allowance.*

1. Place 1 **square** on 1 **rectangle** and stitch diagonally as shown in Fig. 1. Trim 1/4" from stitching line as shown in Fig. 2. Press open, pressing seam allowance toward brown fabric.
2. Place a matching **square** on opposite end of **rectangle**. Stitch diagonally as shown in Fig. 3. Trim 1/4" from stitching line as shown in Fig. 4. Press open, pressing seam allowance toward brown fabric (Fig. 5).
3. Repeat Steps 1 and 2 to make 672 Flying Geese Units.

Fig. 1

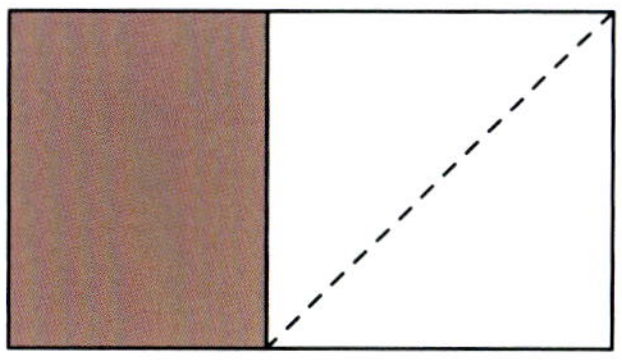

Fig. 2

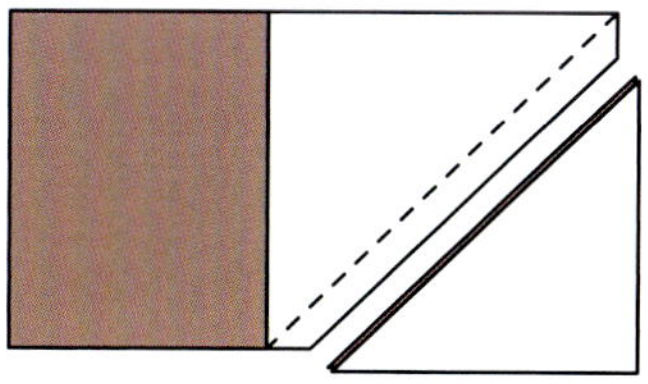

Fig. 3

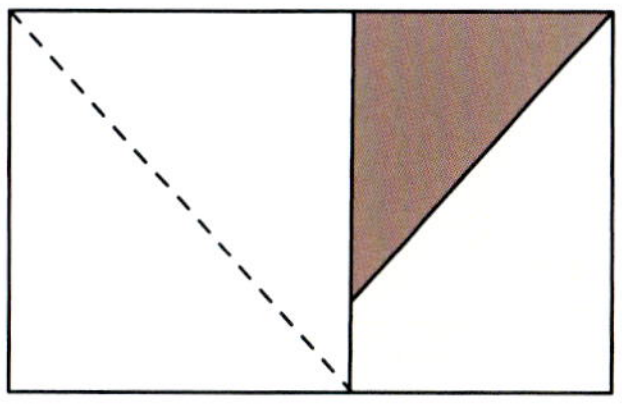

Fig. 4

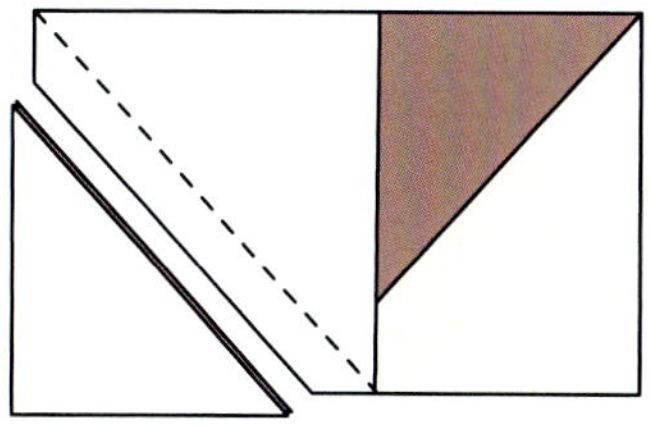

Fig. 5

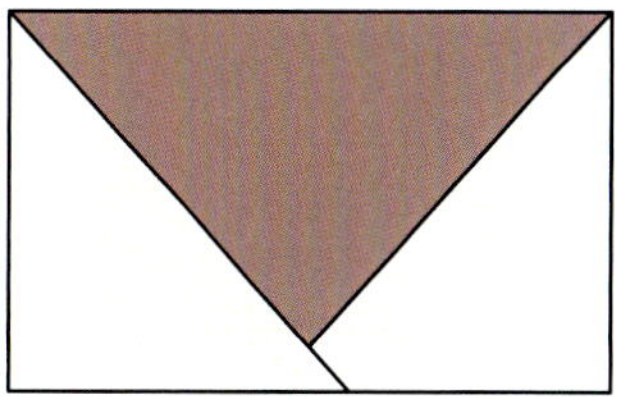

Flying Geese Unit (make 672)

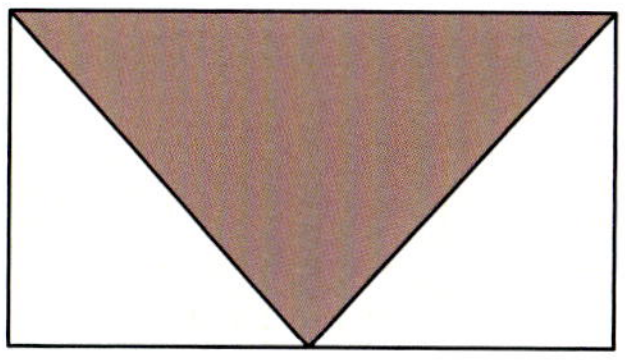

4. Assemble 12 **Flying Geese Units** to make Flying Geese Sashing Strip. Make 56 Flying Geese Sashing Strips.
5. Follow Assembly Diagram to assemble **setting squares**, **side** and **corner setting triangles**, **Flying Geese Sashing Strips**, **sashing squares**, and **side** and **corner sashing triangles** into rows; sew rows together to complete center section of quilt top.
6. Follow Adding Squared Borders, page 41, and Quilt Top Diagram to add **top**, **bottom**, and then **side inner borders**. Add **top**, **bottom**, and then **side outer borders** to complete **Quilt Top**.

Flying Geese Sashing Strip
(make 56)

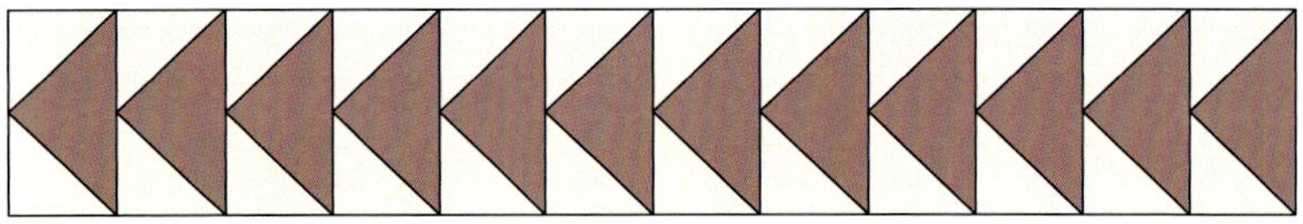

Assembly Diagram

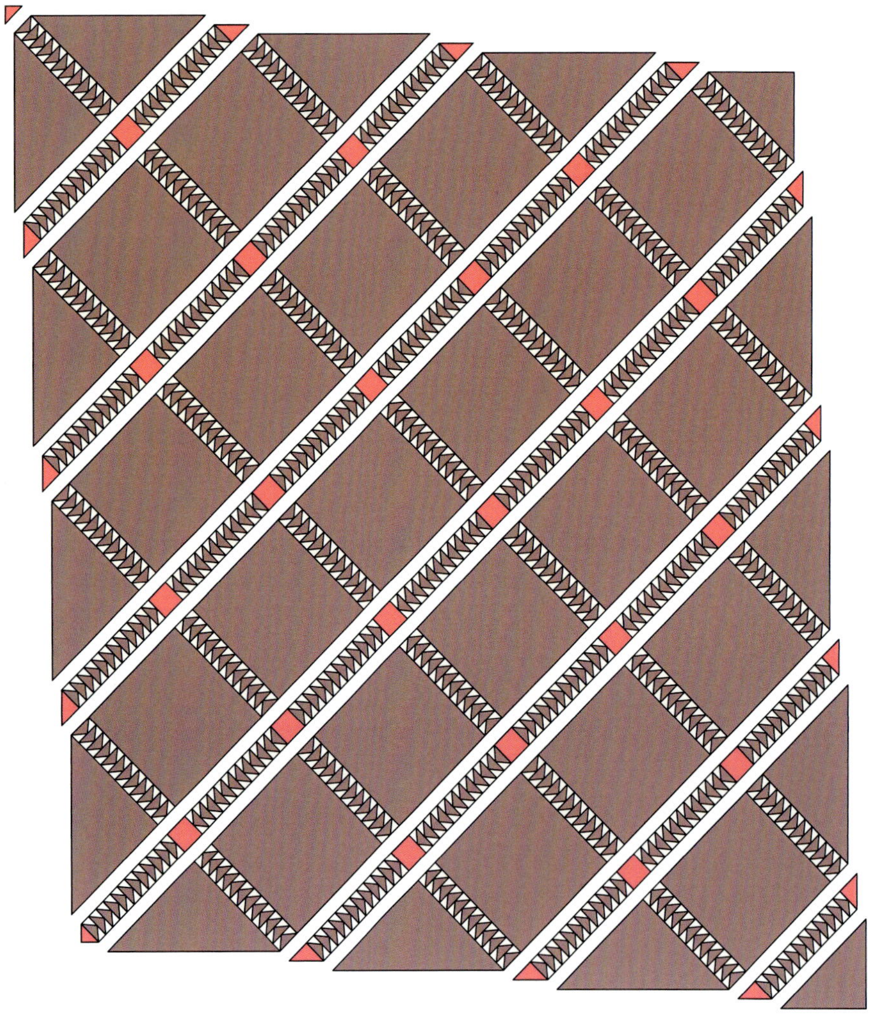

COMPLETING THE QUILT

1. Follow Quilting, page 42, to mark, layer, and quilt. Our quilt is quilted with diagonal crosshatch quilting in the center and straight-line quilting in the center of each border.
2. Cut a 32" square of binding fabric. Follow Binding, page 46, to bind quilt using $2^1/_2$"w bias binding with mitered corners.

Quilt Top Diagram

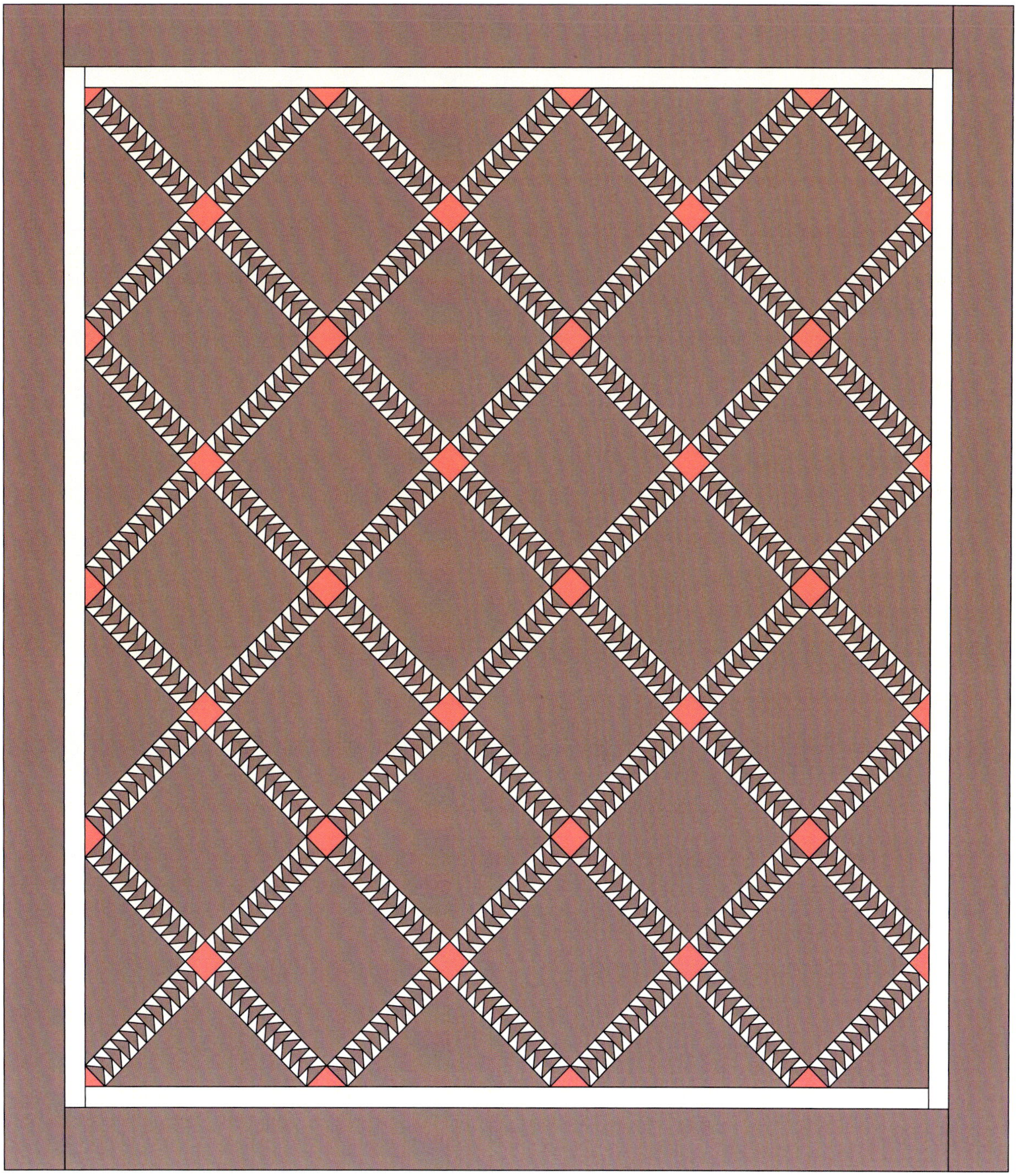

sawtooth quilt

Softly hued and elegant, this quilt will be a joy to its lucky owner for many years to come. "Sawtooth" doesn't really seem to be the best name for such a comforting creation. Other names for the Sawtooth Block used in this design are Road to California, Stepping Stones, and Crossroads, so you can choose the name you like best. The alternating squares with triangles in their corners are super-easy Snowball Blocks.

FINISHED BLOCK SIZE: $10^1/_8$" x $10^1/_8$" (26 cm x 26 cm)
FINISHED QUILT SIZE: $74^3/_8$" x $74^3/_8$" (189 cm x 189 cm)

YARDAGE REQUIREMENTS

Yardage is based on 43"/44" (109 cm/112 cm) wide fabric.

$5^1/_8$ yds (4.7 m) of white solid fabric

$3^1/_4$ yds (3 m) of tan solid fabric

$6^7/_8$ yds (6.3 m) of fabric for backing

1 yd (91 cm) of fabric for binding

$82^3/_8$" x $82^3/_8$" (209 cm x 209 cm) piece of batting

BIRDS

CUTTING THE PIECES

*Follow **Rotary Cutting**, page 40, to cut fabric. Cut all strips across the selvage-to-selvage width of the fabric unless otherwise indicated. All measurements include $\frac{1}{4}$" seam allowances.*

from white solid fabric:

- Cut 4 *lengthwise* **borders** $3\frac{1}{8}$" x $72\frac{3}{8}$".
- From remaining width, cut 16 strips $2\frac{1}{8}$"w. From these strips, cut 192 **A's** $2\frac{1}{8}$" x $2\frac{1}{8}$".
- From remaining width, cut 10 strips $3\frac{7}{8}$"w. From these strips, cut 64 **C's** $3\frac{7}{8}$" x $3\frac{7}{8}$".
- Cut 3 strips $10\frac{5}{8}$" w. From these strips, cut 9 **E's** $10\frac{5}{8}$" x $10\frac{5}{8}$".
- Cut 2 strips $15\frac{5}{8}$" w. From these strips, cut 3 squares $15\frac{5}{8}$" x $15\frac{5}{8}$". Cut each square twice diagonally to make 12 **F's**.
- From remaining width, cut 2 squares $8\frac{1}{8}$" x $8\frac{1}{8}$". Cut each square once diagonally to make 4 **G's**.
- Cut 10 strips $3\frac{5}{8}$" w. From these strips, cut 100 **H's** $3\frac{5}{8}$" x $3\frac{5}{8}$".

from tan solid fabric:

- Cut 11 strips $2\frac{1}{8}$" w. From these strips, cut 192 **A's** $2\frac{1}{8}$" x $2\frac{1}{8}$".
- Cut 7 strips $1\frac{5}{8}$" w. From these strips, cut 64 **B's** $1\frac{5}{8}$" x $3\frac{7}{8}$".
- Cut 2 strips $3\frac{7}{8}$" w. From these strips, cut 16 **C's** $3\frac{7}{8}$" x $3\frac{7}{8}$".
- Cut 6 strips $4\frac{1}{4}$" w. From these strips, cut 48 **D's** $4\frac{1}{4}$" x $4\frac{1}{4}$".
- Cut 10 strips $3\frac{5}{8}$" w. From these strips, cut 100 **H's** $3\frac{5}{8}$" x $3\frac{5}{8}$".

ASSEMBLING THE QUILT TOP

*Follow **Machine Piecing**, page 40, and **Pressing**, page 41. Use a $\frac{1}{4}$" seam allowance.*

1. Draw a diagonal line on wrong side of each white **A**. With right sides together place 1 white A on top of 1 tan **A**. Stitch seam $\frac{1}{4}$" from each side of drawn line (Fig. 1).
2. Cut along drawn line and press seam allowances to darker fabric to make 2 Small Triangle-Squares. Make 384 Small Triangle-Squares. Trim each Small Triangle-Square to $1\frac{5}{8}$" x $1\frac{5}{8}$".
3. Refer to Unit 1 to sew Small Triangle-Squares and 1 **B** together. Repeat to make 64 Unit 1's.
4. Sew 1 **Unit 1** between 2 white **C's** to make Unit 2. Repeat to make 32 Unit 2's. Sew 1 tan **C** between 2 **Unit 1's** to make Unit 3. Make 16 Unit 3's.

Fig. 1

Small Triangle-Squares (make 384)

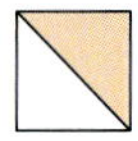

Unit 1 (make 64)

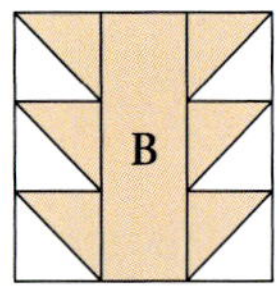

Unit 2 (make 32)

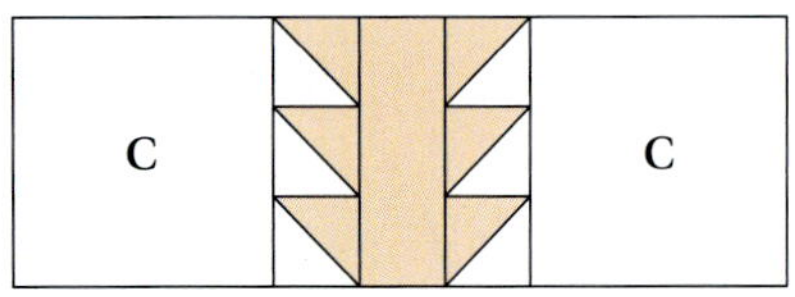

Unit 3 (make 16)

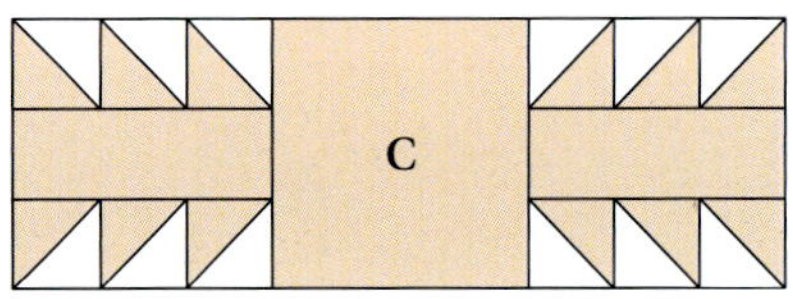

5. Follow **Sawtooth Block** diagram and sew **Unit 3** between 2 **Unit 2's** to complete Sawtooth Block. Make 16 Blocks.
6. Draw a diagonal line on wrong side of each **D**.
7. With right sides together, place 1 D on one corner of 1 **E**. Stitch along drawn line. Trim $^{1}/_{4}$" from stitching line (Fig. 2). Open and press, pressing seam allowances to darker fabric.
8. Repeat for each corner of E to make Snowball Block. Make 9 Snowball Blocks.
9. For each half block, repeat Step 7 to sew 1 **D** to right angle corner of 1 **F**. Repeat to make 12 Half Blocks.
10. Follow Assembly Diagram, page 34, to sew **Sawtooth Blocks**, **Snowball Blocks**, **Half Blocks**, and **G's** together.
11. Trim all sides of quilt top center $^{1}/_{4}$" past outermost corner of blocks.
12. Draw a diagonal line on wrong side of each white **H**. With right sides together place 1 white H on top of 1 tan **H**. Stitch seam $^{1}/_{4}$" from each side of drawn line (Fig. 3).
13. Cut along drawn line and press seam allowances to darker fabric to make 2 Large Triangle-Squares. Make 200 Large Triangle-Squares. Trim each Triangle-Square to $3^{1}/_{8}$" x $3^{1}/_{8}$".
14. For top inner border, follow Quilt Top Diagram, page 35, and sew 22 large triangle-squares together. Repeat to make bottom border. For side inner border, sew 24 large triangle-squares together. Repeat to make a total of 2 side borders. Easing in any fullness, sew inner borders to top, bottom, and sides of assembled blocks.

Sawtooth Block (make 16)

Fig. 2

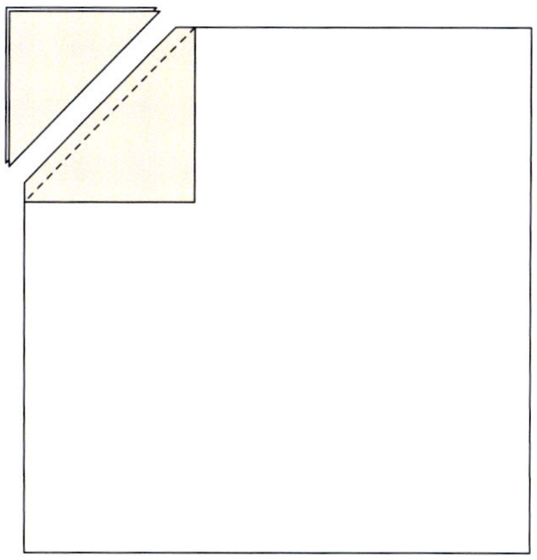

Snowball Block (make 9)

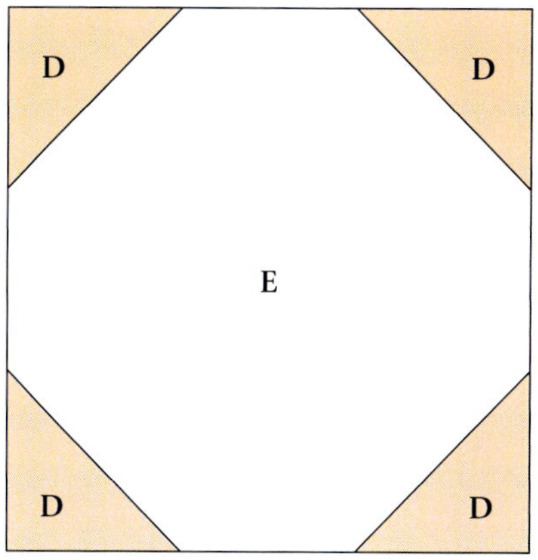

Half Block (make 12)

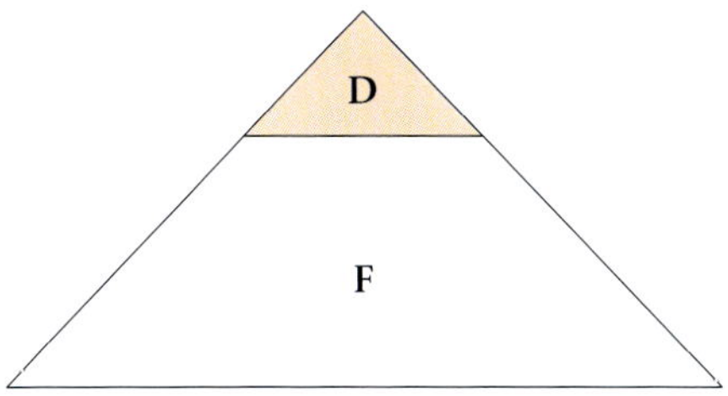

Fig. 3

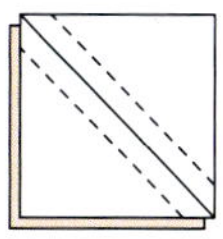

Large Triangle-Squares (make 200)

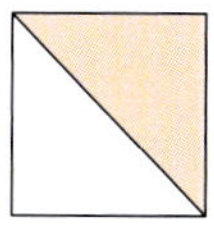

15. Follow Adding Mitered Borders, page 42, to add **borders** to inner border.
16. For top outer border, follow Quilt Top Diagram and sew 26 **Large Triangle-Squares** together. Repeat to make bottom border. For side outer border, sew 28 **Large Triangle-Squares** together. Repeat to make 2 side borders. Easing in any fullness, sew outer borders to top, bottom, and sides of mitered borders to complete **Quilt Top**.

COMPLETING THE QUILT

1. Follow Quilting, page 42, to mark, layer, and quilt. Our quilt is hand quilted with a feathered wreath in each Snowball Block and crosshatch quilting in each Sawtooth Block. The borders are quilted in diagonal lines.
2. Cut a 30" square of binding fabric. Follow Binding, page 46, to bind quilt using $2^1/_2$"w bias binding with overlapped corners.

Assembly Diagram

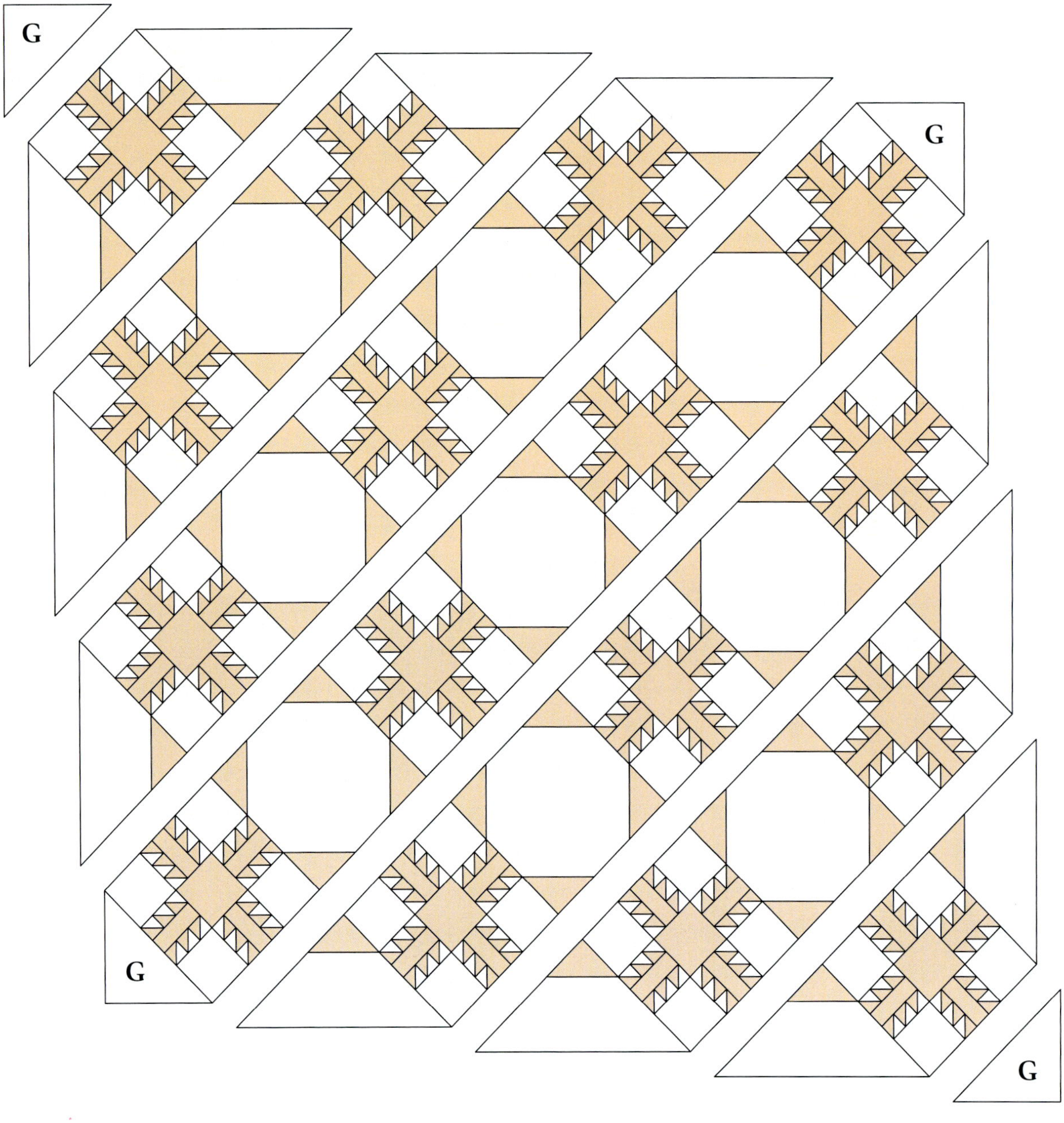

Quilt Top Diagram

friendship album quilt

Most historical sources tell us that album quilts were originally created for future brides by their friends. Album quilts usually include patches of light-color fabrics for signing with ink or embroidery. The Friendship Album blocks in this quilt are simplicity itself, just rectangles and squares to sew together. Today, a Friendship Album quilt would also make a great gift for a student going away to college.

FINISHED BLOCK SIZE: 12 1/2" x 12 1/2" (32 cm x 32 cm)
FINISHED QUILT SIZE: 73 1/2" x 90 1/2" (187 cm x 230 cm)

YARDAGE REQUIREMENTS

Yardage is based on 43"/44" (109 cm/112 cm) wide fabric with a usable width of 40" (102 cm).

2 5/8 yds (2.4 m)
of blue print fabric

5/8 yd (57 cm)
of blue check fabric

1/8 yd (11 cm) **each**
of 20 light print fabrics

1/8 yd (11 cm) **each**
of 20 dark print fabrics

6 7/8 yds (6.3 m)
of fabric for backing

1 yd (91 cm)
of fabric for binding

81 1/2" x 98 1/2"
(207 cm x 250 cm)
piece of batting

CUTTING THE PIECES

Follow ***Rotary Cutting****,* *page 40**, to cut fabric. Cut all strips across the selvage-to-selvage width of the fabric. All measurements include 1/4" seam allowances.*

from blue print fabric:

- Cut 17 strips 5"w. From these strips, cut 49 **sashing strips** 5" x 13".

from blue check fabric:

- Cut 4 strips 5"w. From these strips, cut 30 **sashing squares** 5" x 5".

from each light print fabric:

- Cut 1 strip 3"w. From this strip, cut 10 **squares** 3" x 3".
- Cut 1 **rectangle** 3" x 8".

from each dark print fabric:

- Cut 1 strip 3"w. From this strip, cut 12 **squares** 3" x 3".

ASSEMBLING THE QUILT TOP

*Follow **Machine Piecing**, page 40, and **Pressing**, page 41. Use a $^1/_4$" seam allowance.*

1. Sew 1 light **rectangle**, 10 light, and 12 dark **squares** together to make **Block**. Make 20 Blocks.

Block (make 20)

2. Sew 4 **Blocks** and 5 **sashing strips** together to make **Row**. Make 5 Rows.

Row (make 5)

3. Sew 5 **sashing squares** and 4 **sashing strips** together to make **Sashing Row**. Make 6 Sashing Rows.

Sashing Row (make 6)

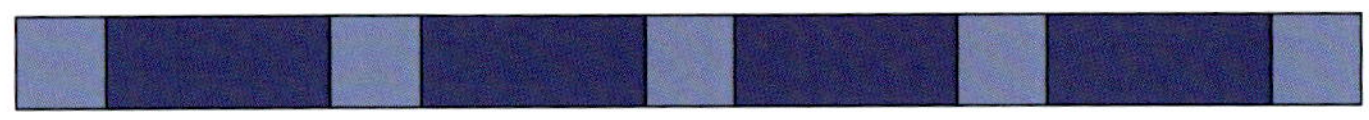

4. Referring to **Quilt Top Diagram**, sew **Rows** and **Sashing Rows** together to complete **Quilt Top**.

COMPLETING THE QUILT

1. Follow **Quilting**, page 42, to mark, layer, and quilt as desired. Our quilt is machine quilted with a flower in the blocks, an "X" in the sashing squares, and parallel lines in the sashings.
2. Cut a 31" square of binding fabric. Follow **Making Continuous Bias Strip Binding**, page 46, to make $2^1/_2$"w bias binding.
3. Follow **Attaching Binding With Mitered Corners**, page 46, to attach binding to quilt.

Quilt Top Diagram

general instructions

To make your quilting easier and more enjoyable, we encourage you to carefully read all of the general instructions, study the color photographs, and familiarize yourself with the individual project instructions before beginning a project.

FABRICS

SELECTING FABRICS

Choose high-quality, medium-weight 100% cotton fabrics. All-cotton fabrics hold a crease better, fray less, and are easier to quilt than cotton/polyester blends.

Yardage requirements listed for each project are based on 43"/44" wide fabric with a "usable" width of 40" after shrinkage and trimming selvages. Actual usable width will probably vary slightly from fabric to fabric. Our recommended yardage lengths should be adequate for occasional re-squaring of fabric when many cuts are required.

PREPARING FABRICS

We recommend that all fabrics be washed, dried, and pressed before cutting. If fabrics are not pre-washed, washing the finished quilt will cause shrinkage and give it a more "antiqued" look and feel. Bright and dark colors, which may run, should always be washed before cutting. After washing and drying fabric, fold lengthwise with wrong sides together and matching selvages.

ROTARY CUTTING

Rotary cutting has brought speed and accuracy to quiltmaking by allowing quilters to easily cut strips of fabric and then cut those strips into smaller pieces.

- Place fabric on work surface with fold closest to you.
- Cut all strips from the selvage-to-selvage width of the fabric unless otherwise indicated in project instructions.
- Square left edge of fabric using rotary cutter and rulers (Figs. 1 - 2).

Fig. 1

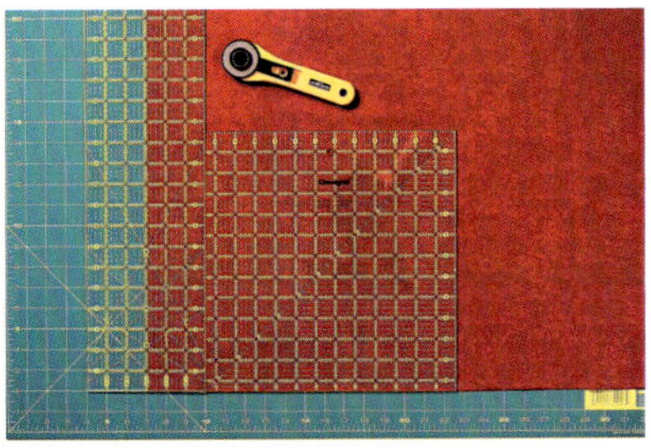

Fig. 2

- To cut each strip required for a project, place ruler over cut edge of fabric, aligning desired marking on ruler with cut edge; make cut (Fig. 3).

Fig. 3

- When cutting several strips from a single piece of fabric, it is important to make sure that cuts remain at a perfect right angle to the fold; square fabric as needed.

MACHINE PIECING

Precise cutting, followed by accurate piecing, will ensure that all pieces of quilt top fit together well.

- Set sewing machine stitch length for approximately 11 stitches per inch.
- Use neutral-colored general-purpose sewing thread (not quilting thread) in needle and in bobbin.

- An accurate $^1/_4$" seam allowance is *essential*. Presser feet that are $^1/_4$" wide are available for most sewing machines.

- When piecing, always place pieces right sides together and match raw edges; pin if necessary.

- Chain piecing saves time and will usually result in more accurate piecing.

- Trim away points of seam allowances that extend beyond edges of sewn pieces.

SEWING STRIP SETS

When there are several strips to assemble into a strip set, first sew strips together into pairs, then sew pairs together to form strip set. To help avoid distortion, sew seams in opposite directions (Fig. 4).

Fig. 4

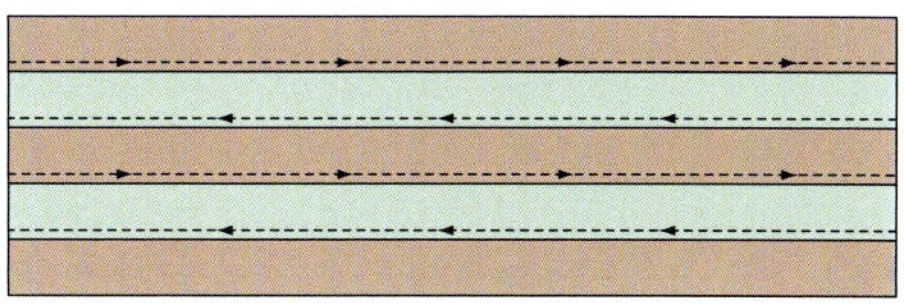

SEWING ACROSS SEAM INTERSECTIONS

When sewing across intersection of two seams, place pieces right sides together and match seams exactly, making sure seam allowances are pressed in opposite directions (Fig. 5).

Fig. 5

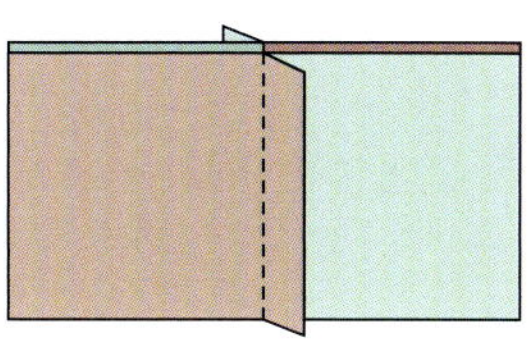

SEWING SHARP POINTS

To ensure sharp points when joining triangular or diagonal pieces, stitch across the center of the "X" (shown in pink) formed on wrong side by previous seams (Fig. 6).

Fig. 6

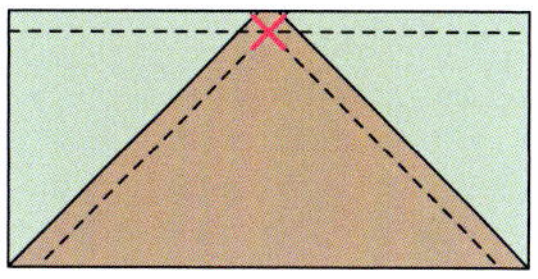

PRESSING

- Use steam iron set on "Cotton" for all pressing.

- Press after sewing each seam.

- Seam allowances are almost always pressed to one side, usually toward darker fabric. However, to reduce bulk it may occasionally be necessary to press seam allowances toward the lighter fabric or even to press them open.

- To prevent dark fabric seam allowance from showing through light fabric, trim darker seam allowance slightly narrower than lighter seam allowance.

- To press long seams, such as those in long strip sets, without curving or other distortion, lay strips across width of the ironing board.

BORDERS

Borders cut along the lengthwise grain will lay flatter and smoother than borders cut along the crosswise grain. Lengthwise-grain borders are especially important for bed-size quilts, since the more stable lengthwise grain is less likely to stretch out of shape and cause wavy edges. Our instructions for cutting borders for bed-size quilts also include an extra 2" at each end for "insurance"; borders will be trimmed after measuring completed center section of quilt top. And, as always, you should match right sides and raw edges and use a $^1/_4$" seam allowance when sewing.

ADDING SQUARED BORDERS

1. Mark the center of each edge of quilt top.
2. Squared borders are usually added to top and bottom, then side edges of the center section of a quilt top. To add top border, measure across center of quilt top to determine length of border (Fig. 7). Trim border to the determined length.

Fig. 7

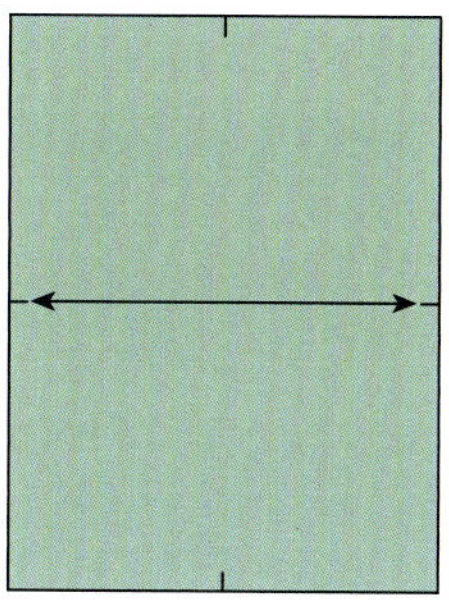

3. Mark center of 1 long edge of border. Matching center marks and raw edges, pin border to quilt top, easing in any fullness; stitch.

4. Repeat Steps 2 and 3 to add bottom border to quilt top.
5. Measure across center of quilt top (including attached borders) to determine length of side borders. Repeat Steps 2 and 3 to add side borders to quilt top (Fig. 8).

Fig. 8

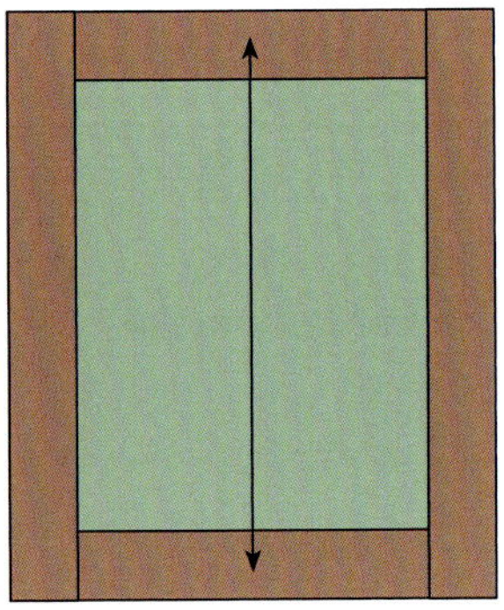

ADDING MITERED BORDERS

1. Mark the center of each edge of quilt top (see Fig. 7).
2. Mark center of 1 long edge of top border. Measure across center of quilt top (see Fig. 7). Matching center marks and raw edges, pin border to center of quilt top edge. From center of border, measure out 1/2 the width of the quilt top in both directions and mark. Match marks on border with corners of quilt top and pin. Easing in any fullness, pin border to quilt top between center and corners. Sew border to quilt top, beginning and ending seams exactly 1/4" from each corner of quilt top and backstitching at beginning and end of stitching (Fig. 9).

Fig. 9

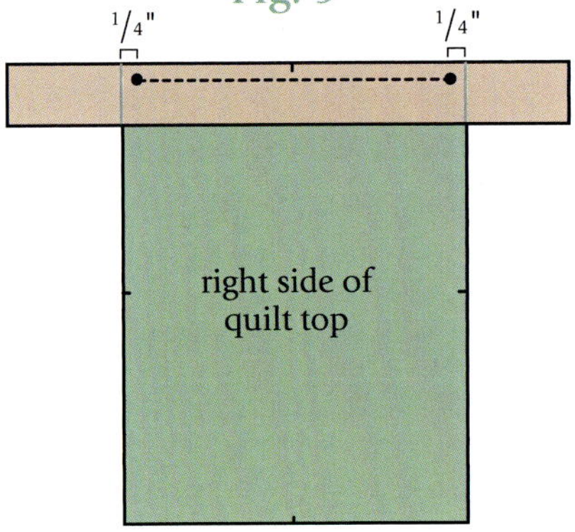

3. Repeat Step 2 to sew bottom, then side borders, to center section of quilt top. To temporarily move first 2 borders out of the way, fold and pin ends as shown in Fig. 10.

Fig. 10

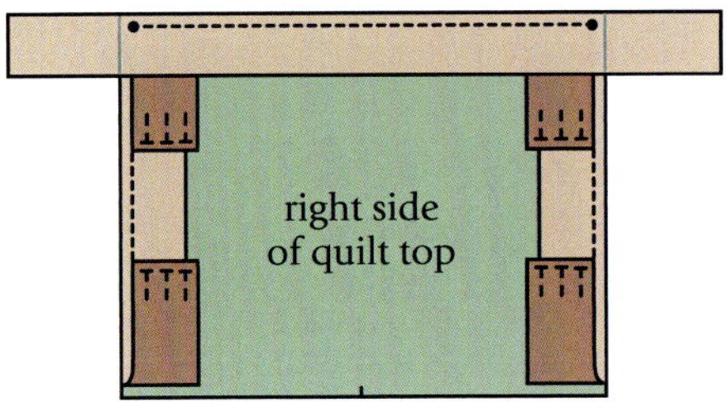

4. Fold 1 corner of quilt top diagonally with right sides together; use rotary cutting ruler to mark stitching line as shown in Fig. 11. Pin strips together along drawn line. Sew on drawn line, backstitching at beginning and end of stitching (Fig. 12).

Fig. 11

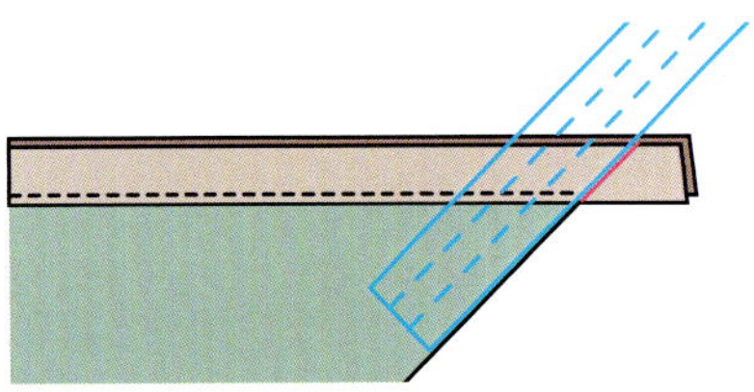

Fig. 12

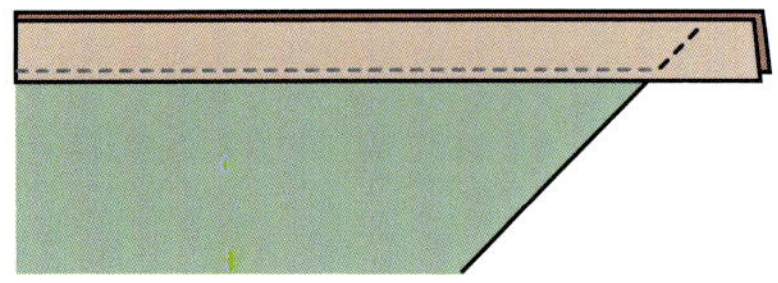

5. Turn mitered corner right side up. Check to see that there is not a gap at the inner end of the seam and that corner does not pucker.
6. Trim seam allowances to 1/4"; press to 1 side.
7. Repeat Steps 4-6 to miter each remaining corner.

QUILTING

Quilting holds the three layers (top, batting, and backing) of the quilt together and can be done by hand or machine. Because marking, layering, and quilting are interrelated and may be done in different orders depending on circumstances, please read entire ***Quilting*** *section, pages 42 – 46, before beginning project.*

MARKING QUILTING LINES

Quilting lines may be marked using fabric marking pencils, chalk markers, water- or air-soluble pens, or lead pencils.

Simple quilting designs may be marked with chalk or chalk pencil after basting. A small area may be marked, then quilted, before moving to next area to be marked. Intricate designs should be marked before basting using a more durable marker.

Caution: Pressing may permanently set some marks. **Test** different markers **on scrap fabric** to find one that marks clearly and can be thoroughly removed.

A wide variety of pre-cut quilting stencils, as well as entire books of quilting patterns, are available. Using a stencil makes it easier to mark intricate or repetitive designs.

To make a stencil from a pattern, center template plastic over pattern and use a permanent marker to trace pattern onto plastic. Use a craft knife with single or double blade to cut channels along traced lines (Fig. 13).

Fig. 13

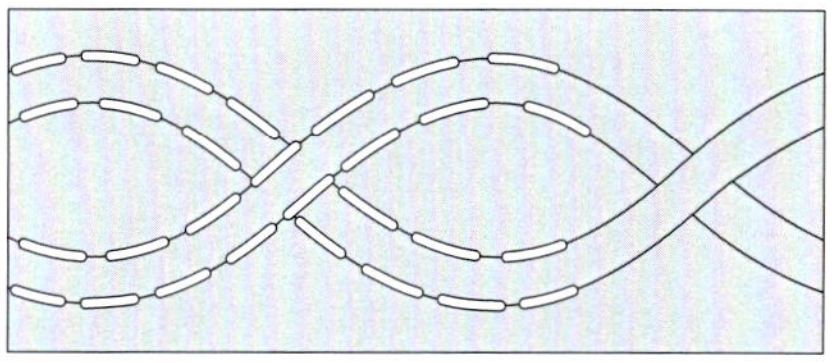

PREPARING THE BACKING

To allow for slight shifting of quilt top during quilting, backing should be approximately 4" larger on all sides. Yardage requirements listed for quilt backings are calculated for 43"/44"w fabric. Using 90"w or 108"w fabric for the backing of a bed-sized quilt may eliminate piecing. To piece a backing using 43"/44"w fabric, use the following instructions.

1. Measure length and width of quilt top; add 8" to each measurement.
2. If determined width is $79^1/_2$" or less, cut backing fabric into two lengths slightly longer than determined *length* measurement. Trim selvages. Place lengths with right sides facing and sew long edges together, forming tube (Fig. 14). Match seams and press along one fold (Fig. 15). Cut along pressed fold to form single piece (Fig. 16).

Fig. 14

Fig. 15

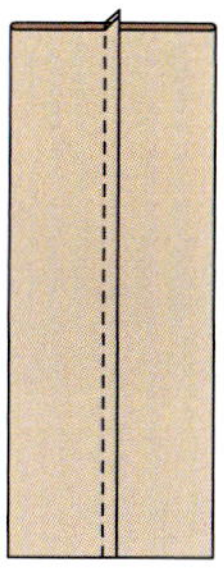

Fig. 16

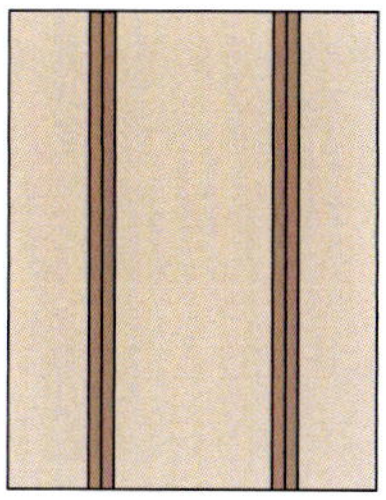

3. If determined width is more than $79^1/_2$", it may require less fabric yardage if the backing is pieced horizontally. Divide determined *length* measurement by 40" to determine how many widths will be needed. Cut required number of widths the determined *width* measurement. Trim selvages. Sew long edges together to form single piece.
4. Trim backing to size determined in Step 1; press seam allowances open.

CHOOSING THE BATTING

The appropriate batting will make quilting easier. For fine hand quilting, choose low-loft batting. All cotton or cotton/polyester blend battings work well for machine quilting because the cotton helps "grip" quilt layers. If quilt is to be tied, a high-loft batting, sometimes called extra-loft or fat batting, may be used to make quilt "fluffy."

Types of batting include cotton, polyester, wool, cotton/polyester blend, cotton/wool blend, and silk.

When selecting batting, refer to package labels for characteristics and care instructions. Cut batting same size as prepared backing.

ASSEMBLING THE QUILT

1. Examine wrong side of quilt top closely; trim any seam allowances and clip any threads that may show through front of the quilt. Press quilt top, being careful not to "set" any marked quilting lines.
2. Place backing *wrong* side up on flat surface. Use masking tape to tape edges of backing to surface. Place batting on top of backing fabric. Smooth batting gently, being careful not to stretch or tear. Center quilt top *right* side up on batting.
3. If hand quilting, begin in center and work toward outer edges to hand baste all layers together. Use long stitches and place basting lines approximately 4" apart (Fig. 17). Smooth fullness or wrinkles toward outer edges.

Fig. 17

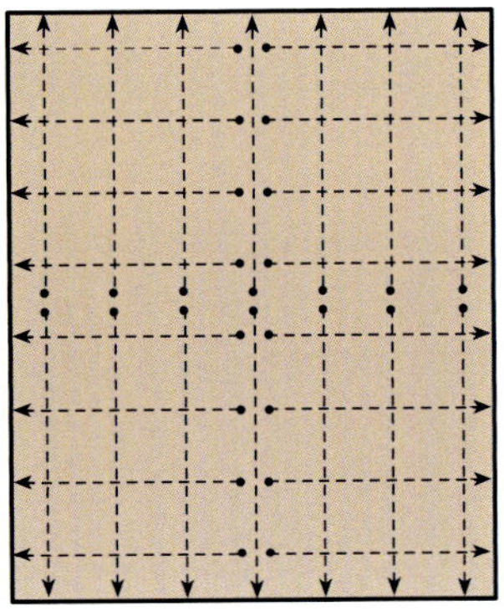

4. If machine quilting or tying a quilt, use 1" rustproof safety pins to "pin-baste" all layers together, spacing pins approximately 4" apart. Begin at center and work toward outer edges to secure all layers. If possible, place pins away from areas that will be quilted, although pins may be removed as needed when quilting.

TYING A QUILT

Tied quilts use yarn or floss ties instead of quilting stitches to secure the layers. For a tied quilt, be sure to use bonded batting to prevent separation or bunching when the quilt is laundered. You may also use a highter loft batting than when quilting.

1. Determine where ties will be placed and mark if necessary. Space ties evenly. On a pieced top, tie at corners of blocks or pieces within blocks.
2. Refer to Preparing the Backing, page 43, and Assembling the Quilt, to prepare quilt for tying.
3. Thread a large darning needle with a long length of embroidery floss, yarn, or pearl cotton; do not knot.
4. At each mark or tie location, take a small stitch through all layers of quilt. Pull up floss, but do not cut between stitches (Fig. 18). Begin at center of quilt and work toward outside edges, rethreading needle as necessary.

Fig. 18

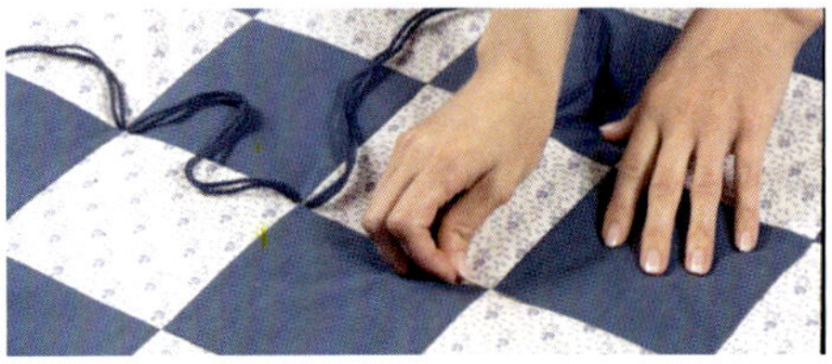

5. Cut floss between stitches. At each stitch, use a square knot to tie floss securely (Fig. 19); trim ties to desired length.

Fig. 19

HAND QUILTING

The quilting stitch is a basic running stitch that forms a broken line on quilt top and backing. Stitches on quilt top and backing should be straight and equal in length.

1. Secure center of quilt in hoop or frame. Check quilt top and backing to make sure they are smooth. To help prevent puckers, always begin quilting in the center of quilt and work toward outside edges.
2. Thread needle with an 18" - 20" length of quilting thread; knot one end. Using thimble, insert needle into quilt top and batting approximately $^1/_2$" from quilting line. Bring needle up on quilting line (Fig. 20); when knot catches on quilt top, give thread a quick, short pull to "pop" knot through fabric into batting (Fig. 21).

Fig. 20

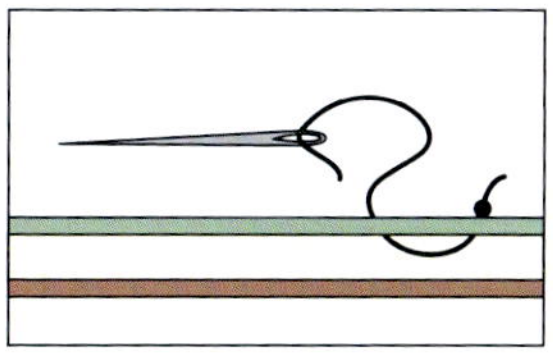

Fig. 21

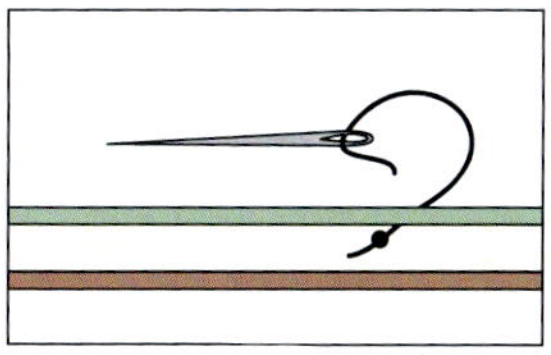

3. Holding needle with sewing hand and placing other hand underneath quilt, use thimble to push tip of needle down through all layers. As soon as needle touches finger underneath, use that finger to push tip of needle only back up through layers to top of quilt. (The amount of needle showing above fabric determines length of quilting stitch.) Referring to Fig. 22, rock needle up and down, taking three to six stitches before bringing needle and thread completely through layers. Check back of quilt to make sure stitches are going through all layers. If necessary, make one stitch at a time when quilting through seam allowances or along curves and corners.

Fig. 22

4. At end of thread, knot thread close to fabric and "pop" knot into batting; clip thread close to fabric.
5. Move hoop as often as necessary. Thread may be left dangling and picked up again after returning to that part of quilt.

MACHINE QUILTING METHODS

Use general-purpose thread in bobbin. Do not use quilting thread. Thread the needle of machine with general-purpose thread or transparent monofilament thread to make quilting blend with quilt top fabrics. Use decorative thread, such as a metallic or contrasting-color general-purpose thread, to make quilting lines stand out more.

Straight-Line Quilting

The term "straight-line" is somewhat deceptive, since curves (especially gentle ones) as well as straight lines can be stitched with this technique.

1. Set stitch length for six to ten stitches per inch and attach a walking foot to sewing machine.
2. Determine which section of quilt will have longest continuous quilting line, oftentimes the area from center top to center bottom. Keeping fabrics smooth, roll up and secure each edge of quilt to help reduce the bulk. Smaller projects may not need to be rolled.
3. Begin stitching on longest quilting line, using very short stitches for the first $^1/_4$" to "lock" quilting. Stitch across project, using one hand on each side of walking foot to slightly spread fabric and to guide fabric through machine. Lock stitches at end of quilting line.
4. Continue machine quilting, stitching longer quilting lines first to stabilize quilt before moving on to other areas.

Free-Motion Quilting

Free-motion quilting may be free form or may follow a marked pattern.

1. Attach a darning foot to sewing machine and lower or cover feed dogs.
2. Position quilt under darning foot; lower foot. Holding top thread, take a stitch and pull bobbin thread to top of quilt. To "lock" beginning of quilting line, hold top and bobbin threads while making three to five stitches in place.

3. Use one hand on each side of darning foot to slightly spread fabric and to move fabric through the machine. Even stitch length is achieved by using smooth, flowing hand motion and steady machine speed. Slow machine speed and fast hand movement will create long stitches. Fast machine speed and slow hand movement will create short stitches. Move quilt sideways, back and forth, in a circular motion, or in a random motion to create desired designs; do not rotate quilt. Lock stitches at end of each quilting line.

BINDING

Binding encloses the raw edges of quilt. Because of its stretchiness, bias binding works well for binding projects with curves or rounded corners and tends to lie smooth and flat in any given circumstance. Binding may also be cut from straight lengthwise or crosswise grain of fabric.

MAKING CONTINUOUS BIAS STRIP BINDING

Bias strips for binding can simply be cut and pieced to desired length. However, when a long length of binding is needed, the "continuous" method is quick and accurate.

1. Cut square from binding fabric the size indicated in project instructions. Cut square in half diagonally to make two triangles.
2. With right sides together and using 1/4" seam allowance, sew triangles together (Fig. 23); press seam allowances open.

Fig. 23

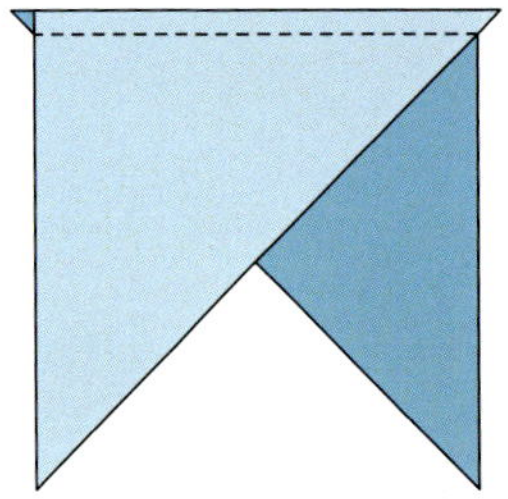

3. On wrong side of fabric, draw lines the width of binding as specified in project instructions, usually 2 1/2" (Fig. 24). Cut off any remaining fabric less than this width.

Fig. 24

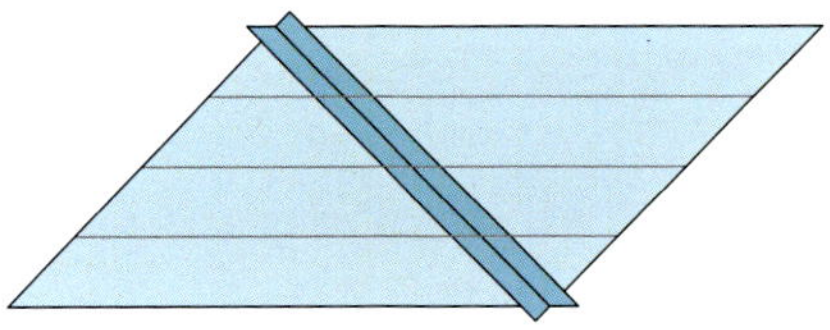

4. With right sides inside, bring short edges together to form tube; match raw edges so that first drawn line of top section meets second drawn line of bottom section (Fig. 25).

Fig. 25

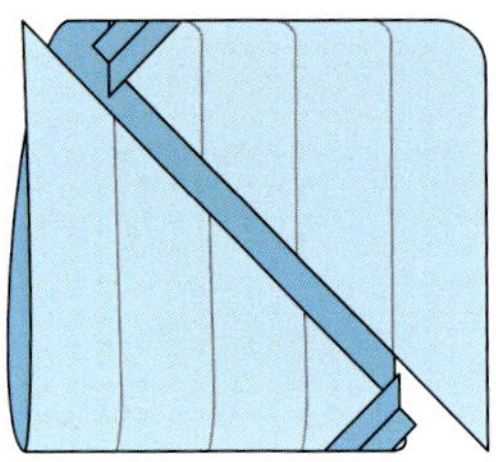

5. Carefully pin edges together by inserting pins through drawn lines at point where drawn lines intersect, making sure pins go through intersections on both sides. Using 1/4" seam allowance, sew edges together; press seam allowances open.
6. To cut continuous strip, begin cutting along first drawn line (Fig. 26). Continue cutting along drawn line around tube.

Fig. 26

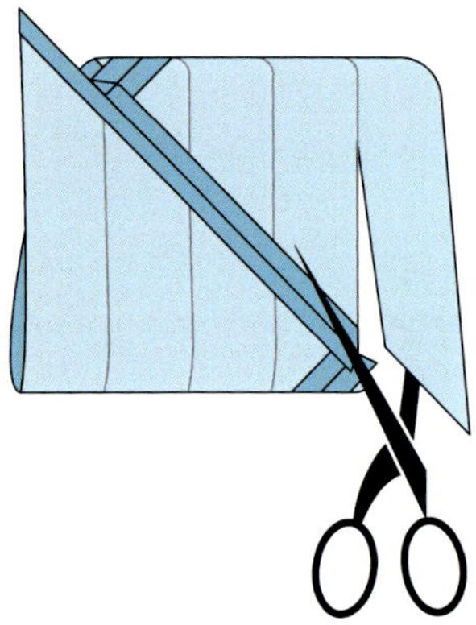

7. Trim ends of bias strip square.
8. Matching wrong sides and raw edges, carefully press bias strip in half lengthwise to complete binding.

ATTACHING BINDING WITH MITERED CORNERS

1. Beginning with one end near center on bottom edge of quilt, lay binding around quilt to make sure that seams in binding will not end up at a corner. Adjust placement if necessary. Matching raw edges of binding to raw edge of quilt top, pin binding to right side of quilt along one edge.

2. When you reach first corner, mark 1/4" from corner of quilt top (Fig. 27).

Fig. 27

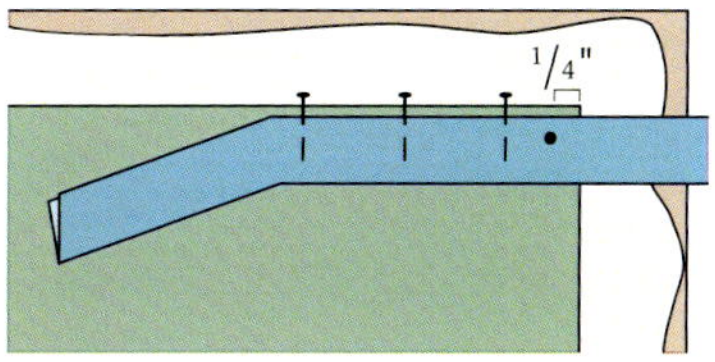

3. Beginning approximately 10" from end of binding and using 1/4" seam allowance, sew binding to quilt, backstitching at beginning of stitching and at mark (Fig. 28). Lift needle out of fabric and clip thread.

Fig. 28

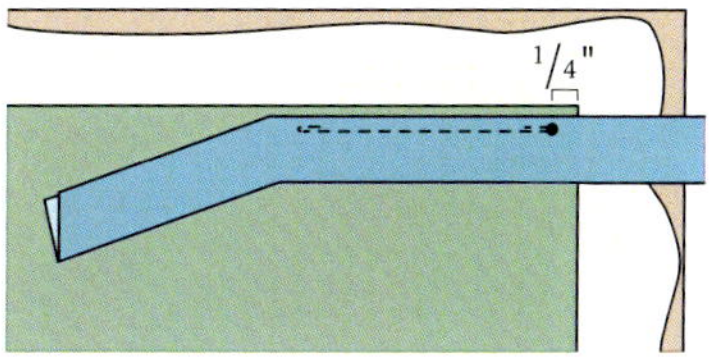

4. Fold binding as shown in Figs. 29 – 30 and pin binding to adjacent side, matching raw edges. When you've reached the next corner, mark 1/4" from edge of quilt top.

Fig. 29

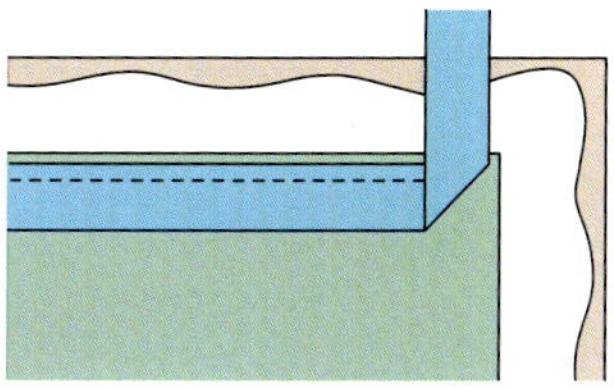

Fig. 30

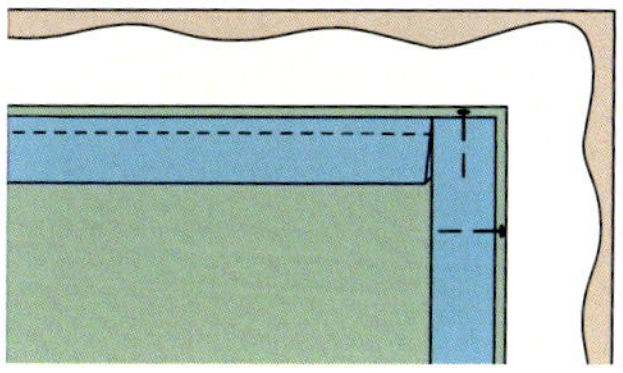

5. Backstitching at edge of quilt top, sew pinned binding to quilt (Fig. 31); backstitch at the next mark. Lift needle out of fabric and clip thread.

Fig. 31

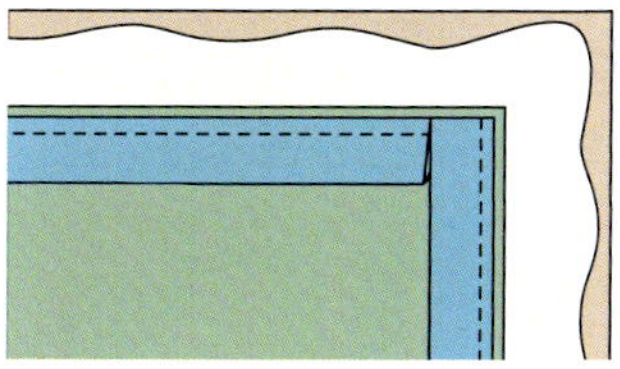

6. Continue sewing binding to quilt, stopping approximately 10" from starting point (Fig. 32).

Fig. 32

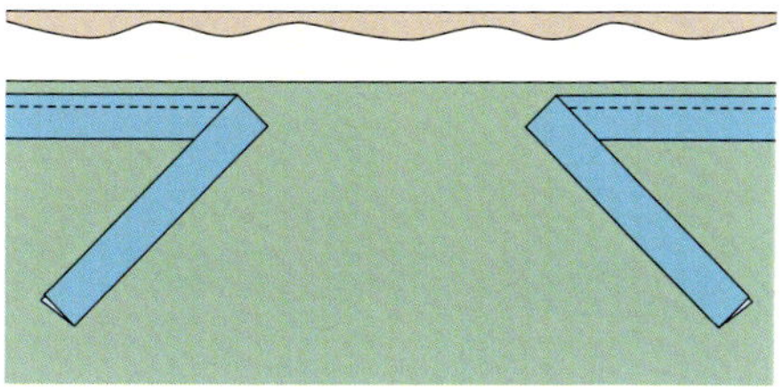

7. Bring beginning and end of binding to center of opening and fold each end back, leaving a 1/4" space between folds (Fig. 33). Finger press folds.

Fig. 33

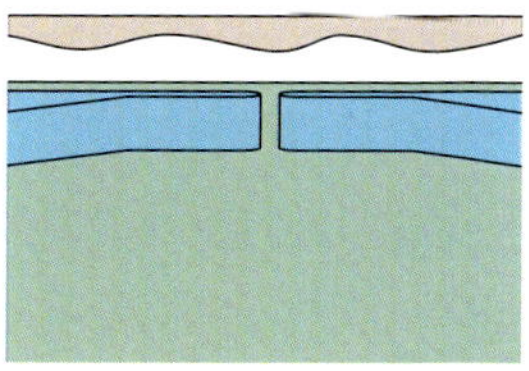

8. Unfold ends of binding and draw a line across wrong side in finger-pressed crease. Draw a line through the lengthwise pressed fold of binding at the same spot to create a cross mark. With edge of ruler at cross mark, line up 45° angle marking on ruler with one long side of binding. Draw a diagonal line from edge to edge. Repeat on remaining end, making sure that the two diagonal lines are angled the same way (Fig. 34).

Fig. 34

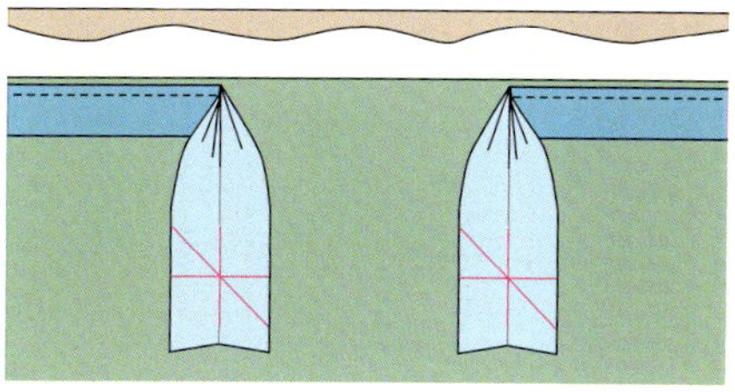

9. Matching right sides and diagonal lines, pin binding ends together at right angles (Fig. 35).

Fig. 35

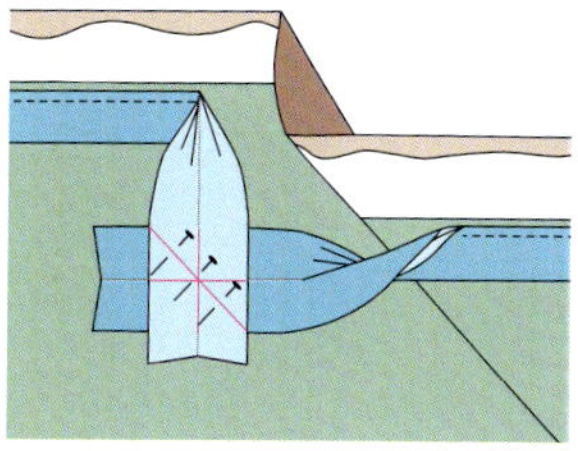

10. Machine stitch along diagonal line (Fig. 36), removing pins as you stitch.

Fig. 36

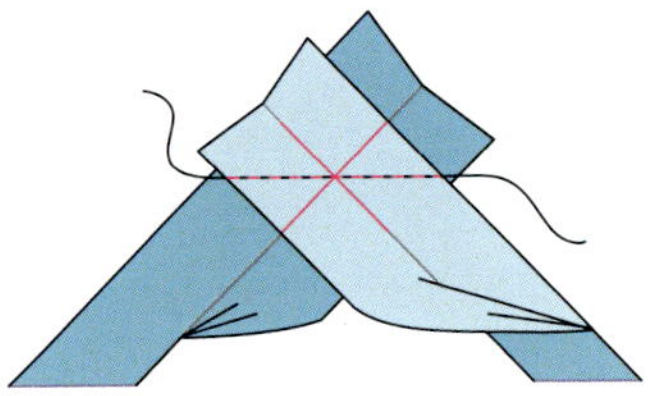

11. Lay binding against quilt to double check that it is correct length.
12. Trim binding ends, leaving 1/4" seam allowance; press seam open. Stitch binding to quilt.
13. Trim backing and batting a scant 1/4" larger than quilt top so that batting and backing will fill the binding when it is folded over to quilt backing.
14. On one edge of quilt, fold binding over to quilt backing and pin pressed edge in place, covering stitching line (Fig. 37). On adjacent side, fold binding over, forming a mitered corner (Fig. 38). Repeat to pin remainder of binding in place.

Fig. 37

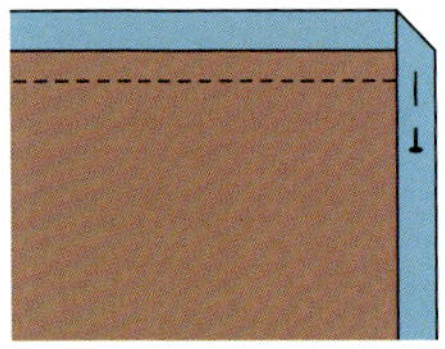

Fig. 38

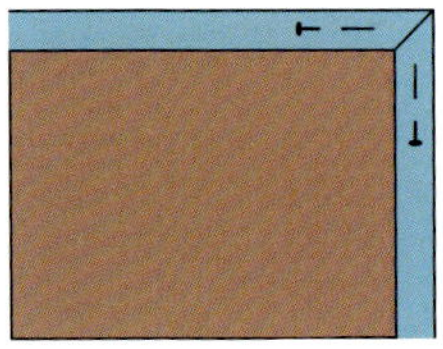

15. Blindstitch binding to backing, taking care not to stitch through to front of quilt.

ATTACHING BINDING WITH OVERLAPPED CORNERS

1. Measure each edge of quilt top; add 3". Cut 1 length of binding for each determined measurement.
2. Matching raw edges and using 1/4" seam allowance, sew a length of binding to top and bottom edges on right side of quilt.
3. Trim backing and batting from top and bottom edges a scant 1/4" larger than quilt top so that batting and backing will fill the binding when it is folded over to quilt backing.
4. Trim ends of top and bottom binding even with edges of quilt top. Fold binding over to quilt backing and pin pressed edges in place, covering stitching line (Fig. 39); blindstitch binding to backing.

Fig. 39

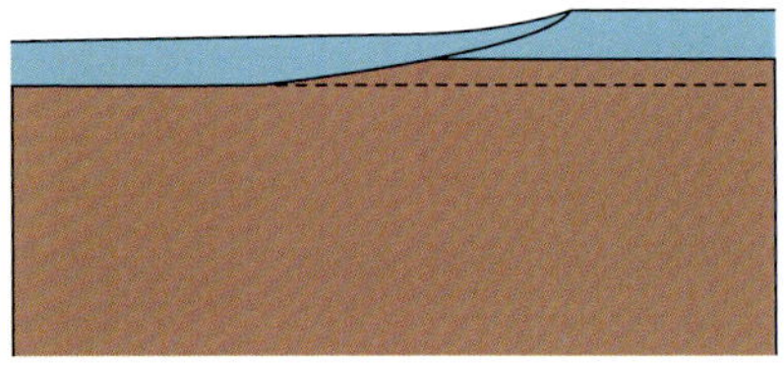

5. Leaving approximately 1 1/2" of binding at each end, stitch a length of binding to each side edge of quilt. Trim backing and batting as in Step 3.
6. Trim each end of binding 1/2" longer than bound edge. Fold each end of binding over to quilt backing (Fig. 40); pin in place. Fold binding over to quilt backing and blindstitch in place, taking care not to stitch through to front of quilt.

Fig. 40

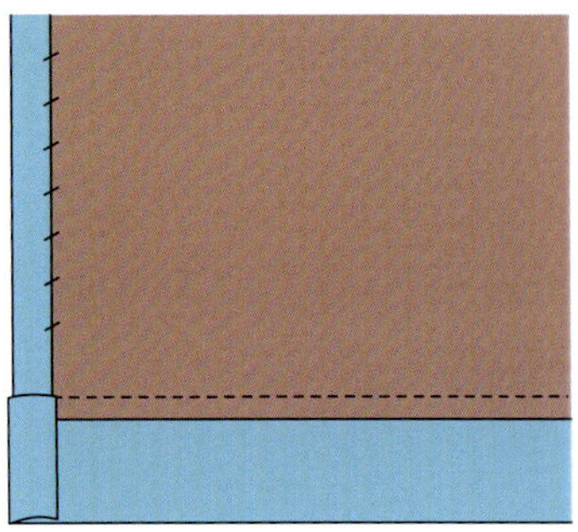

Metric Conversion Chart

Inches x 2.54 = centimeters (cm)	Yards x .9144 = meters (m)
Inches x 25.4 = millimeters (mm)	Yards x 91.44 = centimeters (cm)
Inches x .0254 = meters (m)	Centimeters x .3937 = inches (")
	Meters x 1.0936 = yards (yd)

Standard Equivalents

1/8"	3.2 mm	0.32 cm	1/8 yard	11.43 cm	0.11 m
1/4"	6.35 mm	0.635 cm	1/4 yard	22.86 cm	0.23 m
3/8"	9.5 mm	0.95 cm	3/8 yard	34.29 cm	0.34 m
1/2"	12.7 mm	1.27 cm	1/2 yard	45.72 cm	0.46 m
5/8"	15.9 mm	1.59 cm	5/8 yard	57.15 cm	0.57 m
3/4"	19.1 mm	1.91 cm	3/4 yard	68.58 cm	0.69 m
7/8"	22.2 mm	2.22 cm	7/8 yard	80 cm	0.8 m
1"	25.4 mm	2.54 cm	1 yard	91.44 cm	0.91 m